CONTENTS

Chapter One: An Overview

Chapter Two: The Adoption Debate

Introduction

Adoption is the forty-fifth volume in the **Issues** series. The aim of this series is to offer up-to-date information about important issues in our world.

Adoption looks at the main aspects of the adoption procedure and the current problems.

The information comes from a wide variety of sources and includes:
Government reports and statistics
Newspaper reports and features
Magazine articles and surveys
Literature from lobby groups
and charitable organisations.

It is hoped that, as you read about the many aspects of the issues explored in this book, you will critically evaluate the information presented. It is important that you decide whether you are being presented with facts or opinions. Does the writer give a biased or an unbiased report? If an opinion is being expressed, do you agree with the writer?

Adoption offers a useful starting-point for those who need convenient access to information about the many issues involved. However, it is only a starting-point. At the back of the book is a list of organisations which you may want to contact for further information.

*****

Adoption – some questions answered

Information from the British Agencies for Adoption & Fostering (BAAF)

What is adoption?

Adoption is a way of providing new families for children who cannot be brought up by their own parents. It is a legal procedure in which all the parental responsibility is transferred to the adopters. Once an adoption order has been granted and the time limit for lodging an appeal has expired, it can't be reversed except in circumstances which are extremely rare. An adopted child loses all legal ties with their first mother and father (the 'birth parents') and becomes a full member of the new family, usually taking the family's name.

When most people think of adoption, they think of young babies. But very few young babies are available for adoption nowadays. The wider use of contraception and abortion means that fewer unplanned babies are born, and changes in people's attitudes and increased help from the state have made it easier for single parents to bring up children on their own. In 1995 only 322 children below the age of one were adopted.

However, there are still thousands of people who want to adopt children, and an increasing number of them are now interested in older children. More people are also adopting or fostering children with disabilities and groups of brothers and sisters who would otherwise have to spend their childhood in temporary foster care, children's homes and other institutions. Children like these – older children, children with disabilities, groups of brothers and sisters who need to stay together, and children of minority ethnic groups who need families of the same ethnic background – are often referred to as children with 'special needs'.

What is the difference between adoption and fostering?

Adoption is a legal process by which a child becomes a permanent and full member of a new family. Fostering is a temporary arrangement to allow a child to live with a family until circumstances enable the child to return to their own family, live independently, or be placed for adoption. (Many children are fostered for only a few weeks or months during a family crisis such as illness.)

Unlike adoptive parents, foster carers are always given an allowance towards the cost of keeping the child and in some cases they are also paid for their services. They always share the responsibility for the child with a fostering agency. BAAF's leaflet, *Foster care – some questions answered*, gives further information about fostering.

What kind of people can be adopters?

The law (both in England and Wales and Scotland) requires that people who adopt children must be over 21 and must be able to show that they can give a child the care he or she needs.

However, because there are so few babies available nowadays and so many childless couples who want babies, most of the adoption agencies which arrange this kind of adoption have a wide choice of families and can afford to add further conditions of their own.

These requirements vary from agency to agency and can be hard for couples to meet. For example, most agencies will only place healthy babies with married couples who can prove they are unable to have children of their own. They often give an upper age limit of between 35 and 40; some will not accept people who have been divorced, and most expect the marriage to have lasted for at least three years before they will consider an application to adopt a baby.

When it comes to people who want to adopt children with 'special needs', agencies are much more flexible. These children may settle more happily with older parents who have experience of bringing up children, or perhaps with a single parent who has plenty of time for them, or in a family where there are

already children. It is the needs of the child which are most important.

People who are interested in adoption don't have to be particularly well off, thought naturally adoption agencies make sure that the new family can afford to take in a child. In special cases there are allowances which are available to help meet the costs of bringing up a child.

How do people find a child to adopt?

The first thing to do is to approach an adoption agency. There are nearly 200 in Britain: most are part of local authority social services or social work (in Scotland) departments but some, known as voluntary agencies, are run independently. Some voluntary agencies have connections with particular churches. People who want to adopt a healthy baby may well not be able to, as so few such children need adoption. (BAAF's book, *Adopting a Child*, includes a list of agencies as well as information about adoption procedures and practice.) All adoption agencies are looking for new parents for children with 'special needs'. Sometimes they advertise in local newspapers and other media; they also use family-finding services like Adoption UK's newsletter, BAAF's *Be My Parent* (which publishes details of children needing permanent new families) or BAAFLink, a nationwide computerised linking service.

What about adopting children from abroad?

Sometimes you see heartbreaking pictures of children in distant parts of the world who seem to have no one to care for them. It is natural for people to think about the kind of life these children could have with new adoptive parents in this country, and many people who are not able to adopt a baby in Britain consider looking overseas.

It is necessary to have a home study done by a local authority. However, there is no adoption agency in Britain which brings children into the country so would-be adopters have to make their own arrangements and deal with many legal complications. Governments of different countries have their own regulations about children leaving their country, and in Britain, Home Office immigration rules also have to be satisfied before a child can enter the country. Then, once the child is here, the adoption process often has to be gone through in a British court. It all takes a lot of time, effort and money.

Quite apart from all these practical difficulties, it is important to consider whether it is right to take children away from their country of birth and bring them into an alien culture. Many people feel that it would be better to provide resources for these children to stay and be brought up in their own countries. And many governments are unhappy about their children going abroad for adoption. Whatever difficulty a country is experiencing now, its children represent its hopes for the future.

Do all adoptions have to go through an adoption agency?

Unless people are adopting the child of a close relative, or a child who has been living with them for more than one year, they have to go through an adoption agency. This agency, which will be either a local authority or an approved voluntary agency, can make proper enquiries about the suitability of the would-be parents. All adoptions must be agreed by the courts.

Are children 'matched' to their adoptive parents?

Adoption agencies try to follow the wishes of the birth parents when they choose the family a child should go to. For example, some people ask that their black and minority ethnic child should be brought up in a particular religion. Agencies do not usually try to match the physical appearance of the child to that of the new parents. However, agencies now agree that, wherever possible, a child should be brought up in a family of the same ethnic background as the birth parents. Children who are adopted by parents of another ethnic group may feel cut off from their roots, whereas families from the same background, for example, black and minority ethnic families, are more able to give black and minority ethnic children a sense of cultural identity and to help them cope with the racial prejudice they may meet.

When adoption agencies are finding homes for older children with developed personalities, they look for families who can encourage their individual interests and talents. And children with physical or learning disabilities or emotional difficulties need parents with particular strengths.

How does an adoption become legal?

An adoption does not become legal until a court makes an adoption order transferring all the birth parents' parental responsibility to the child's adoptive parents. Once this order is made, it usually cannot be reversed and the birth parents no longer have any legal connection with the child although in some cases they may stay in touch and have some form of contact.

Before this happens, social workers from the adoption agency spend a lot of time talking with all the people involved. First, they will talk with the birth parents about what they think is rights for their child. They will want to learn as much as possible about the family in order to make the right plans for the child's future. If the child is old enough, the social worker will want to know what he or she thinks about the adoption plan.

Next, the social workers will spend a lot of time getting to know the would-be adopters. The agency will want to find out what sort of parents they are likely to be and to help them prepare for the special job of being adoptive parents. In particular, they have to check on adoptive parents' backgrounds, for instance, their medical histories and whether they have been in trouble with the police.

If the agency considers the family suitable to adopt, the child will go to live with them. After that, they can apply to court for an adoption order. The court cannot make an adoption order until the child has lived with the adopters for a least 13 weeks. This period does not start until the child is six weeks old, so no order is ever made before a child is 19 weeks old. The birth parents are asked to agree to the adoption order being made. If they are married, both of them are asked to agree but if they are not, only the mother will be asked.

The court appoints a special person, a Reporting Officer, who checks that the birth parents understand what adoption is about and witnesses their agreement to the adoption order being made. If the birth parents do not agree to adoption, the adopters can ask the court to make an order without agreement. The court can only do this in special circumstances, for instance, if the child has been abandoned. An independent worker called a guardian *ad litem* (in Scotland, a curator *ad litem*) will be appointed by the court to enquire into the situation and advise the court on whether an adoption order should be made.

There is also another sort of court order, called a 'freeing order'. This allows birth parents to 'free' their children for adoption by transferring their parental responsibility to the adoption agency. The adoption agency holds this respons-ibility until it can be transferred to the child's adoptive parents, by the court making an adoption order.

Freeing means that the birth parents can get their part of the adoption finished without too much delay, even when it may not be possible for the adoption order to be made for some time.

What happens at the adoption hearing?

If the child's parents agree to the adoption taking place, the hearing in court usually lasts less than half an hour. The judge or magistrates read a report prepared by social workers from the adoption agency, then ask the prospective parents a few questions and give their decision immediately.

If the adoption is contested by the birth parents, it is best if all concerned have legal advice, including the potential adopters. The court hearing is likely to be much longer and more complicated and will involve the independent worker (guardian *ad litem* in England and Wales or curator *ad litem* in Scotland) reporting to the court on what is best for the child.

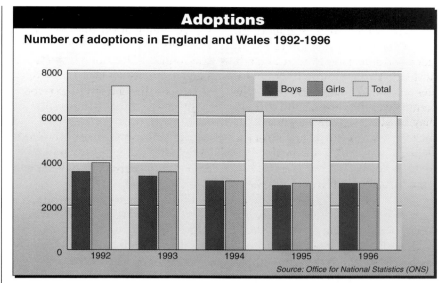

Adoptions

Number of adoptions in England and Wales 1992-1996

Source: Office for National Statistics (ONS)

What rights do birth parents have?

Parents usually have the right to decide whether their child is to be adopted. The mother is asked to sign a document giving her agreement and, if the parents were married to each other when the child was born, the father must give his permission as well. In other cases, the father is not asked for his agreement although he should be consulted and, in some circumstances, must be given the chance to propose alternatives to adoption for the court to consider. In exceptional circumstances, the court may decide that the parents are behaving unreasonably in refusing to agree, and can overrule them if they feel that this will be best for the child.

The adoption agency has a duty to consult the birth parents about the kind of family their child should be placed with, although it may not be able to carry out all their wishes. If the birth mother and the new adoptive parents wish, it may be possible for them to meet.

The parents of the child being adopted can change their minds at any stage up to the time when the adoption order is granted. In this case, the court will hear the evidence of a guardian *ad litem* or a curator ad litem on what is best for the child. If the child is already happily settled with the potential adoptive parents, the court may decide that the adoption should go ahead regardless. Once the adoption order has been granted, the birth parents have no further rights over the child.

What does adoption cost?

Adoption agencies do not charge a fee and it is illegal for any money to pass from the adopters to the child's birth parents. Any payment of this kind would normally mean that the couple could not legally adopt the child in question. Some voluntary agencies are run as charities and people may feel that they want to make a donation, although this will not affect their chances of being accepted as potential adopters.

Sometimes they may also be asked to contribute towards the agency's expenses, for example, travel costs. People adopting a baby usually have to pay for their medical examination and meet court charges, but these are usually small.

Prospective adopters should ask the agency for details of its policy with regard to expenses such as these. They also need to be aware that if the application is contested in court they will need legal advice and almost certainly legal representation. In a small number of cases the legal costs could be very high. If it is known before a child is placed that an application is likely to be contested, most agencies will agree to meet the reasonable legal costs of the adopters, although they may expect them to attempt to obtain legal aid first.

In other cases that become contested unexpectedly (for example, because a birth parent withdraws her or his agreement) agencies' policies will vary.

Once an adoption order has been granted the new parents take on complete financial responsibility for the upkeep of the child. Like any other parents, they will be able to receive child benefit and other state benefits. If an adoptive child has special needs which involve the parents in extra expense – perhaps for medical treatment – the parents may be able to receive an adoption allowance which will help them meet these costs. This allowance is arranged by the adoption agency.

Adoption agencies (except voluntary societies which have made it clear that they do not pay adoption allowances) will give information to adopters about allowances and the way in which they are calculated. In some circumstances it may be appropriate for an agency (particularly a local authority) to make a maintenance payment for the period between placement and the making of an adoption order. Families can claim child benefit from the date on which a child is placed with them under adoption regulations.

Do birth parents and other relatives have any contact with their child after adoption?

It is unusual for face-to-face contact to be maintained when a child is adopted as a baby, although the two families may exchange photographs and letters by mutual agreement. Older children who remember their birth family may want to maintain some level of contact with them. If the adoption agency and both the birth parents and the adopting parents are happy about this, it can be arranged.

How much are adopting parents told about the child's background?

The adoption agency gives the adopting parents as much information as possible about the health, origins, background and experiences of the child and of the birth parents. This helps them to be good and understanding parents and also enables them to satisfy the child's natural curiosity about him or herself.

Should children be told they are adopted?

Yes. How and when a child is first told depends on the adopting family and the child's level of understanding, but in general the advice is: the earlier the better. Then as the child grows older and becomes better able to understand, most families explain in more detail.

Experience has taught is that it is much easier for a child to grow up with the knowledge of his or her adoption than to make the discovery later on. BAAF's book, *Talking about adoption to your adopted child*, gives much more information.

Do adopted children want to trace their birth parents?

Most adopted children are curious about their origins, but this does not mean that they do not love their adoptive parents so new parents should not feel threatened by this curiosity. The Children Act 1975 gave adopted people in England and Wales the right to see their birth certificates and know more about their origins when they reach the age of 18; in Scotland the age is 16 and this right has existed since legal adoption was first introduced.

The original birth certificate gives the mother's name, occupation, date of the child's birth and address at the time of the child's birth. It may also give similar details about the father. If the adoption happened before November 1975, the certificate is given to the adopted person by a trained counsellor, who can also help the adopted person to find out which agency arranged the adoption and contact the agency. This is not the situation in Scotland and adopted people seeking access to their birth records have no statutory requirements to seek counselling. It is assumed that new parents of children adopted after that will have been helped by their adoption agency to prepare the child for receiving this extended knowledge. Some people are satisfied with the fuller knowledge and understanding gained in this way, while others feel the need to try to trace their original parents or other birth family members.

What about adoption by step-parents?

Sometimes step-parents want to adopt the children from the previous marriage of their new husband or wife. If this happens, the child's legal links with their other birth parents and wider family will be broken. Alternative ways of settling the child's situation are often better – see BAAF's leaflets, *Stepchildren and adoption*, in England and Wales and Scotland.

© *British Agencies for Adoption and Fostering (BAAF)*

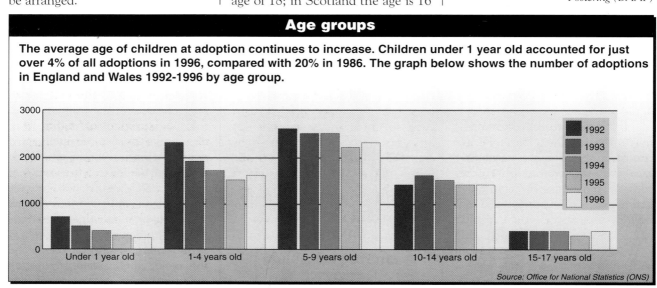

Age groups

The average age of children at adoption continues to increase. Children under 1 year old accounted for just over 4% of all adoptions in 1996, compared with 20% in 1986. The graph below shows the number of adoptions in England and Wales 1992-1996 by age group.

Source: Office for National Statistics (ONS)

Adoption, fostering and residential care

Adoption has changed a great deal over the last generation. Single mothers rarely give up their children for adoption these days just because they are single, so consequently there are hardly any new-born babies needing adoptive parents. However, adoption is still very important in providing families for children who for various reasons cannot live with their own birth parents and need a permanent substitute family.

Children who need a 'for ever' family may be:

- Any age, but often over five years
- From various religious, cultural and ethnic backgrounds
- Children with physical or learning disabilities
- Children who have had many changes in their lives
- Children who have been emotionally, physically or sexually abused
- Groups of brothers and sisters who need to stay together
- Children who, although they need a new permanent family, need to maintain some links with members of their birth family.

Could you become an adoptive parent?

Because the children needing adoptive families are so varied, all kinds of people are needed to care for them. You could be:
- Married or single
- With or without other children
- Of any age or racial background

If you have love to share, time to spare and plenty of patience and energy, do contact CCWC or your local society to find out more, without the slightest obligation. Being an adoptive parent certainly isn't easy, but you will be given plenty of preparation and ongoing help and support for as long as you need it after a child has joined your family.

The Catholic Children's Societies and adoption

Twelve of the seventeen Catholic agencies in England are registered adoption agencies; those which are not can refer you to a neighbouring agency which will help you. The agencies for Wales, Scotland and Northern Ireland are also adoption agencies. These Catholic societies have a long history of involvement in adoption and make up about half the voluntary adoption agencies in the UK. Although nowadays not catering exclusively for Catholic children or Catholic adopters, they offer a service which is particularly geared to those for whom faith background is important.

Fostering

Many children need looking after, but because of their circumstances it is not suitable for them to be adopted. A number of the Catholic societies recruit and support foster carers, both long-term and short-term, for such children (including teenagers), who continue to be in the care of a local authority. Carers of a Catholic or other faith background and of a variety of racial mixtures are always welcomed. If you think you could help, read the section above on adoption as there are a lot of similarities, without the final commitment of adoption.

Residential care

In the past, there were a large number of children in Catholic residential care (some 18,000 in Catholic children's homes around 1950), but with changes in practice these homes have mainly closed. However, there is a minority of children for whom residential care is the most suitable option, and six of our societies (in the dioceses of Southwark, Liverpool, Salford, Lancaster, Leeds and Hexham & Newcastle) run children's homes, which offer various specialised services, with a Catholic flavour.

Other services for children

Other services offered by various of the Catholic societies include:
- Day care for children with physical or learning disabilities
- Respite care for children with physical or learning disabilities
- Mother and baby homes and assessment centres
- Guardian-ad-Litem services

© Catholic Child Welfare Council

Thinking about adoption

Twenty questions to ask yourself before applying to adopt a child

1. First of all it is a good idea to try to put yourself in the shoes of the social worker. Remember that he or she should be concerned above all else with the interests and needs of the child. Of course, these will be best served if the social worker is able to find parents whose strengths and needs fit those of the child. That is why you may be asked what may seem to be very searching questions. Can you accept this intrusion and make it a positive experience? Ideally, what happens should be a joint exploration between you and the social worker.

2. It is very important to recognise your limitations; not hiding your weaknesses but offering your strengths as potential parents. Can you list your strengths and weaknesses and acknowledge them as part of you? You will find this much easier if you can make friends with your social worker. Be hospitable and try to make time to talk about other things; she/he will respond and you will find the whole process much less of an ordeal than you might have anticipated!

3. If you are a couple in a marriage or long-term partnership, the enthusiasm of both partners is essential; an excessively dominant wife or husband who never lets the other half get a word in, is likely to put a social worker off. On the other hand, don't worry if one of you usually does the talking for both; but can you discuss issues of concern openly between you?

4. You must be totally committed to your offer of a place in your family to a child. You may be asked to cease any fertility treatment, or even expected to use contraception during assessment and the settling-in period. This is to avoid any further upheavals for a child who may already have experienced traumatic life events. Can you accept these possible limitations?

5. If you are single, don't let that put you off. Some children need the attention and single-minded commitment of a solo parent. But bear in mind that anyone else in your house over the age of 16 will need to be included in some interviews and to have police and other references taken up. Will they be prepared to do this?

6. If there are already children in your family, a protective feeling towards them is natural and should be respected by a social worker. A newcomer, probably with a very different history and experience, will inevitably cause some difficulties and have an impact on all family members. It is essential that you take some time to consider this and think how it will affect your own children's lives. Think about their ability to cope with difficult behaviour, seek their opinions and listen to their views. How do you think your children will respond to the reality of a newcomer?

7. Currently, it is very unusual for new parents to be considered for a child from different racial, cultural or religious origins to their own. If you are considering a child whose origins differ from your own, remember that as s/he grows up, the outside world will see him/her as 'different'. You will need to have thought through how you are to help your child become a self-confident adult, secure in his/her own identity. Have you given sufficient thought to the implications and impact on you and your family of becoming a mixed-race family?

8. Many of the children placed for adoption today have had traumatic experiences early in life; these may include loss, abuse, or neglect and are likely to imply long-term special needs, at school as well as at home. Moreover, you may be thinking of adopting a child with a specific disability or a particular educational need. It is very important to find out as much as you can about the services and schools available locally and it will help you to learn much more about helping children with particular problems. Look out for voluntary support groups in your area for children with specific disabilities and make contact early, so that you will have all the information and encouragement available. Adoption UK can let you have a list of useful addresses of such groups. There is no substitute for talking to others who have experienced the same problems. Will you also have the support of your wider family and friends in the long term?

9. Having a tidy, well-organised home is not a requirement for adoption. A child who has experienced a lot of change may feel more comfortable in a relaxed environment, where a little organised chaos is not a crisis! However, everyone has their limits, and it is important to work out where yours are. Routine, structure and boundaries may be important for a child who has never experienced these, but rigidity may be frightening or simply too hard to manage. At times your patience will be sorely tested. How adaptable and resilient are you?

10. Integrating a new child into a family is never problem free. One difficulty often experienced by couples is that their child may relate positively to one parent but behave in a hostile way towards the other. This can be very hard to bear and needs a lot of tolerance and understanding by both parents. It is essential that parents provide a united approach and support each other at all times. Is your marriage or partnership one where you can really talk things through and support one another through major problems of this sort?

11. All children changing families have faced serious disruption in their lives. Some who have had months or years of distress or uncertainty may take a very long time to trust you enough to put down new roots. Some may be so hurt by their early experiences that they can never wholly trust you and will not be able to give back the love and affection you offer them. This can be very hard to cope with but Adoption UK can offer you advice and support. Could you remain patient and committed if you have to wait for trust and affection to grow?

12. All adopted children come with roots and family histories which will be different to your own. Could you make it your responsibility to collect and gradually share with a child the details of his/her past life to help him/her build a secure future with you, founded on reality?

13. Social workers will be glad to know of stressful situations with which you have coped and survived; there is no better way to assess the strength of a marriage. Adopting a child can put a great strain on relationships which cannot be imagined beforehand. This much-wanted child may reject you as parents and test you beyond all normal limits. Your expectations may be of a normal, loving family life but reality might be more like a battle ground! It is important to work out ahead of time just what you can cope with and how adaptable your lifestyle is. Be sure about the strength of your partnership and your future plans and hopes. Misunderstandings can lead to placement breakdown with sub-sequent pain for all concerned, espe-cially the child. Can you be open and honest with each other and discuss with your social worker the implica-tions of impending moves, job changes or problems in the relationship?

14. Social workers are dreadfully put off by know-alls, even more so than by those who hardly respond at all! Be careful, and remember that some of the worst offenders are other professionals! Are you one of these?

15. It is really helpful to do a bit of background reading. You may well be given books to read and discuss between visits. We hope you will

find our booklist and journals helpful. We can also, almost always, put you in touch, through our Experience Resource Bank (ERBIE), with other adoptive parents who have struggled with the same questions you are facing and who may be able to offer advice and encouragement from their experiences. Adopted children have special needs as a result of their life experience and you are likely to need help and advice from time to time as your child grows up. Sometimes you may need professional intervention to manage specific problems. Are you hoping to be an 'ordinary' family leading an independent life, or will you be able to seek and accept the help you may need in parenting these very special children?

16. Once an agency has taken up your application for adoption, your social worker will be obliged by law to take up police and local authority references. You will also have to provide two referees for your social worker to talk to, and to have a full medical report. None of these need alarm you as they are simply legal and commonsense requirements for all agencies responsible for the placement of children in new families. How do you feel about sharing such confidential parts of your life?

17. When your new child joins your family s/he will need to feel comfortable in your neighbourhood. How will your friends, neighbours and wider family react to his/her arrival, and help him/her feel welcome?

18. Try and be honest and objective about yourself and face up to the things which you would find very hard to cope with; we are all human, but in different ways! Talk to other adoptive parents about what they have found difficult and read as much as you can. It is not just behaviour issues that cause problems but also the feelings of rejection and failure when things do not go as planned. Think about how you would handle these feelings and consider where your weak spots are, because your child will surely find them! How well do you know yourself?

19. Having a sense of humour is a great help in achieving happy parenthood. Can you laugh at yourself and with others?

20. Many people have an 'ideal vision' about what is involved in family life which they or their children can rarely live up to! Life is never quite what we plan or expect. Children are wonderful but each is an individual who may not fulfil your fantasies. Can you be content with 'less than perfection'?

Don't panic if you can't answer all these question confidently. We are all human and children need parents not paragons!

• For help and encouragement either before or after adoption just contact us at Adoption UK tel: 01327 260295, fax: 01327 263565 or see page 41 for address details.

© Adoption UK
June, 1999

Access to birth records

Information for people adopted in England or Wales

This information explains the provisions in adoption law, chiefly the Adoption Act 1976, under which adopted adults (at least 18 years of age) can apply to the Registrar General for access to the original record of their birth.

Background: Adoptions in England or Wales

In the past it was thought best for all concerned that an adopted child's break with his birth family should be total. Parents who placed a child for adoption were generally told that a child would not have access to his birth record. The current legislation reflects increased understanding of the wishes and needs of adopted people. It recognises that although adoption makes a child a full member of a new family, information about his or her origins may still be important to an adopted person.

People adopted before 12 November 1975 are required to see a counsellor before they can be given access to their records because in the years before 1975, some parents and adopters may have been led to believe that the children being adopted would never be able to find out their original names or the names of their parents. These arrangements were made in good faith and it is important that adopted people who want to find out more about their origins should understand what it may mean for them and for others.

This means that if you were adopted before 12 November 1975, the Adoption Act requires you to see an experienced social worker called a counsellor before you can obtain information from your original birth record.

If you were adopted after 11 November 1975, you may choose whether or not you would like to see a counsellor before you are given the information which will lead you to your birth record. You may find it helpful to see a counsellor as they may be able to offer practical advice and guidance as well as discussing any concerns or issues important to you.

The purpose of counselling

The purpose of counselling is:
- to give adopted people basic information about their adoption in a helpful manner, and
- to help adopted people to understand some of the possible effects on themselves and others of any further enquiries they may wish to make about their birth families.

How and where to apply

You should complete the application form for access to birth records. If you do not already have a form, you can obtain one by writing to the Registrar General at:

Office for National Statistics, The General Register Office, Adoptions Section, Smedley Hydro, Trafalgar Road, Birkdale, Southport PR8 2HH

The form asks you for some details of your adoption so that your Adoption and Birth Registration can be traced.

You should send your completed application form to the above address. When the Registrar General receives your application form he will write to you about the next step. All applications are, of course, treated in strictest confidence.

Places where you can meet a counsellor

You are asked to choose where you would prefer to meet a counsellor. You may choose between:
- The General Register Office;
(The appointment will be arranged at The Family Records Centre, 1 Myddelton Street, London EC1R 1UW. This will be done as quickly as possible but it may take a few weeks.)
- the local authority, regional or island council (Scotland), or Health and Social Services Board (Northern Ireland) in whose area you are living or who made the adoption order;
(The information will be forwarded to the Area Headquarters Office who will then notify the local office nearest to where you are living.)
- any other local authority, council (Scotland) or Board (Northern Ireland); or
- if your adoption was arranged by an approved adoption society, by that society providing it is still operating as an adoption society.

Meeting the counsellor

You will understand that it is very important that precautions are taken against information about you being given to an unauthorised person. To avoid this you must take with you some means of identification, such as a bank card, a passport/identity card or a driving licence.

What the counsellor can tell you

The Registrar General will have sent the counsellor most of the information from your adoption order. This includes:
- your original name;
- the name of your birth mother;
- possibly, but not certainly, the name of your birth father;
- the name of the court where the order was made.

The counsellor will give you this information at your request.

The counsellor will not have a copy of your original birth record at the interview but will be able to give you the necessary application form. You can use the information which the counsellor will give you and the application form to apply for a copy of your original birth record at any time if you decide you want one. There is a statutory fee for this birth certificate.

Birth records

A certificate of birth provides the following information:

- the date and place of your birth;
- the name under which you were originally registered;
- your mother's name and perhaps her occupation;
- the name and address of the person who registered the birth;
- the date of registration;
- the name of the registrar.

It may or may not give your father's name and occupation. If a child's parents are not married to each other, the father's name is not always on the birth certificate.

Further information

Whether or not additional information exists which could be made available to you depends on a number of things, including how your adoption was arranged.

Your adoption could have been arranged through an adoption society or privately. If you were adopted before most private adoption arrangements were prohibited, your adoption could have been arranged through an individual such as a doctor, a solicitor or a friend, or your mother might have arranged it on her own, privately. Some children are adopted by grandparents or other relatives and there have also been a very large number of adoptions by a birth parent with a step-parent.

If your adoption was arranged through an adoption society or a local authority, they may have records. Also, local authorities may have information about adoptions which took place in their area even though they did not arrange them. The counsellor will not have this information but will be able to give you an authorisation to ask the court which made your adoption order for the name of the adoption society or local authority, if any, that took part in the arrangements for your adoption. If the court records are still available and the court is able to give you the name of the adoption society or local authority concerned, you will be able to follow up your enquiries with them. If you were adopted after 12 November 1975 and have decided not to have counselling, you can obtain an authorisation from the Registrar General whose address is given above.

To avoid disappointment, however, it must be said that there can be no certainty that any additional information about your adoption or background still exists. Before 1984, adoption agencies were only required to keep their records for twenty-five years and the court records are not kept indefinitely. Local authorities' records may not go back far enough to include people whose adoption took place many years ago, or they may have been lost or destroyed. However in some instances old papers can be located and your counsellor may be able to advise you about this or give you the address of a post adoption service or organisation which may be able to help you.

Unfortunately, old records are often brief so that information that you may want to have may not be included. However much they want to help, the organisations involved may not, for one reason or another, be able to give you the information you would like.

Although you may not be able to get all the information you would like, these arrangements will make sure that you get some basic facts about your birth mother and perhaps your birth father too.

If you decide not to see a counsellor

If you were adopted after 11 November 1975 and indicate on your application form that you do not wish to see a counsellor, the information will be sent direct to you by the Registrar General. You will receive:

- the name of the court which made the adoption order and the number, if any, of the adoption application;

In the past it was thought best for all concerned that an adopted child's break with his birth family should be total

---

- the name under which you were originally registered;
- the name of your birth mother.

This information will enable you to apply for a copy of your original birth record at any time. There is a statutory fee for this birth certificate.

You will also receive a copy of the authorisation form which will enable you, if you wish, to ask the court which made the adoption order for the name of the local authority or adoption society, if any, that took part in the arrangements for your adoption. Even though you have not seen a counsellor before gaining access to your birth records, a post adoption service will be pleased to offer any support, assistance, or advice you may need, particularly if you decide to contact your birth family.

Adoption contact register for England and Wales

You may be interested to know that the Registrar General also maintains at the General Register Office an Adoption Contact Register, the purpose of which is to put persons adopted in England or Wales and their relatives in touch with each other if this is what they both want.

This article provided information to people adopted in England and Wales and who either continue to live in the UK or are living overseas but who intend to travel to the UK for counselling.

A separate leaflet is available for people living outside the UK who would like to have access to their birth records in their own country. New arrangements were introduced on 14 October 1991 to enable people who were adopted before 12 November 1975 to receive the necessary counselling in the country in which they live.

If your adoption took place in Scotland application for access to birth records should be made to: The Registrar General, New Register House, Edinburgh EH1 3YT

If your adoption took place in Northern Ireland application should be made to: The Registrar General, Oxford House, 49/55 Chichester Street, Belfast BT1 4HL

The Adoption Contact Register

Information for people adopted in England and Wales and their birth relatives

Foreword

1. The Children Act 1989 provides for the Registrar General to operate an Adoption Contact Register. This information explains the background to the introduction of the Register on 1 May 1991 and describes the way it works. There are notes on:

- how to use the Register if you were adopted and how to use it if you are a birth parent or other relative of an adopted person;
- the possibility of using the address of a third party (an intermediary) through which contact can be made;
- what happens when there is a link on the Register between an adopted person and a relative.

For the purposes of the Register, 'relative' includes the adopted person's birth parents and anyone related to that person by blood, half blood or marriage: it does not include those who are relatives as a result of adoption.

Background to the adoption contact register

2. Since 1975 adopted adults have been able to apply for access to their original birth record. This does not change. The information on a birth certificate includes the name of the birth mother and her address at that time: it may have her maiden name, if any, and possibly the name, address and occupation of the birth father. Using this information, some adopted people have been able to trace and make contact with their birth parents or other relatives. But until now there have been few ways of learning whether contact would be welcome. A register provides a safe and confidential way for birth parents and other relatives to assure an adopted person that contact would be welcome and to give a current address.

3. The Register is in two parts. Part I is a list of adopted people and Part II is a list of birth parents and other relatives of an adopted person. The Registrar General will send to an adopted person on the Register the name of any relatives who have also registered, together with the address supplied by the relative, and tell the relative that this has been done. No information about the adopted person can be given to a birth parent or other relative. A registration fee is payable for entry in the Adoption Contact Register.

Important information for users

4. The purpose of the Adoption Contact Register is to put adopted people and their birth parents or other relatives in touch with each other where this is what they both want. Birth parents and other relatives who have decided that they would prefer not to have contact with an adopted person need have no fear that the introduction of the Register will put them at greater risk of an unwanted approach. The Register cannot help an adopted person to learn of the whereabouts of a birth parent or other relative unless that person has chosen to be entered on the Register. The Registrar General can only pass on a name and address if and when that name and address are supplied to him.

5. The introduction of the Register cannot, of course, prevent an adopted person from trying to find a birth

---

A register provides a safe and confidential way for birth parents and other relatives to assure an adopted person that contact would be welcome and to give a current address

---

parent, just as an adopted person can do at present, even though that birth parent has not applied for entry on the Register. If you are worried that an approach from a son or daughter or other relative who was adopted could cause you difficul-ties it may be helpful and reassuring to discuss your anxieties with an experienced counsellor.

6. 'Contact' may have different meanings for different people using the Register. Contact may be assumed by one person to be an open invitation to visit. Another person may see contact as an exchange of information, possibly through a third party and not including any meetings. Between these two extremes there can be many variations. You should be prepared for the possibility that the expectations of the adopted person and the relative may differ.

7. The Registrar General cannot pass letters or any information between adopted people and their relatives, beyond a name and address. However, some relatives may prefer initial contact to be limited to exchanges of letters or information. If this applies to you, you may ask the Registrar General to register you under the address of an organisation which will act as an intermediary between you and the adopted person.

Who can use the register and how it works

Adopted people

8. An adopted person must be at least eighteen years old to use the Register. The Registrar General must hold a record of his or her birth. If the birth took place outside England and Wales, the Adoption Court Order must state the birth particulars.

If, however, the adoption took place in Scotland a separate voluntary service is provided. Information can be obtained from Birth Link, Family Care, 21 Castle Street, Edinburgh EH2 3DN.

9. To be able to complete the application form you will need to have some information about your birth including:

- the name in which your birth was registered before you were adopted
- your date and place (town, village or district) of birth
- your birth mother's name and surname
- your birth mother's maiden name and birth father's name if these were included in your original birth entry.

10. If you do not have this information your adoptive parents may be able to tell you. Otherwise you can apply for access to your birth record. The leaflet *Access to Birth Records: Information for People Adopted in England or Wales* (ACR 100) explains the procedure and can be obtained from the Registrar General at the address given in paragraph 17. A separate leaflet, ACR 101, is available for people living outside the UK who would like to have access to their birth records in their own country. Any adopted adult can be given information about their birth record. This does not depend upon a relative being included on the Adoption Contact Register and no fee is charged.

11. When you are entered on the Register, it may be discovered that a relative has already registered. If this happens you will be sent the name and address supplied by the relative and a note of his or her relationship to you. If no relative has registered you will only receive an acknowledgement of your registration. However, you will be sent details of any relative who subsequently registers. This may happen quite soon or it could be many years later, or may not happen at all.

It is therefore most important that you keep the Registrar General informed of any change of name or address.

Birth parents and other relatives

12. A relative who wishes to be included in Part II (relatives) of the register must provide evidence of his or her relationship to the adopted person. For instance, a birth mother

may easily prove her relationship by providing a copy of her birth certificate, her child's birth certificate, and if she was married after the birth of her child, a copy of her marriage certificate(s). Other relatives may have to provide additional certificates in order to prove their relationship. If certificates are not available, and the birth or marriage occurred in England or Wales, it will be sufficient to provide full details with the application.

13. A birth father who was not married to the baby's mother may not have been included in the original birth record and may have difficulty in proving his relationship to the adopted person. An affiliation or other court order declaring paternity would be acceptable evidence but the absence of such orders need not necessarily prevent entry in Part II of the Register. The Registrar General will be pleased to advise in individual cases.

14. In circumstances where a relative is now using a name different from that in use at the date of birth of the adopted person, other than as a consequence of their marriage(s), the Registrar General will need to examine evidence of the change of name e.g. deed poll or statutory declaration. If no such evidence is

available relatives are asked to notify the Registrar General accordingly and await his advice.

15. To be able to complete an application form and so that the Registrar General may identify your relative who was adopted, you must provide full details of his or her birth. You will need to know:

- the name in which his or her birth was registered before being adopted
- the date and place (town, village or district) of birth
- the birth mother's name
- the birth mother's maiden name and birth father's name if these were included in the original birth entry.

The Registrar General will acknowledge your registration when he has established your relationship to the adopted person and has been able to locate the birth record from the information you supplied.

16. Just as an adopted person cannot receive information from the Register unless a relative has provided information, so the information which a relative has provided cannot be sent to the adopted person unless he or she chooses to register. This could happen quite soon or it could happen after many years or it may not happen at all. Although this may be very disappointing there is no other action which the Registrar

Number of adoptions

There were 6,000 adoptions in England and Wales in 1996, the latest year for which figures are available. This represents an increase of 3% over the 1995 figure.

Source: Office for National Statistics (ONS)

General can take. You may find it helpful to discuss all the implications with a counsellor.

17. Application forms for adopted people and for relatives can be obtained by writing to the Registrar General at:

Office for National Statistics, The General Register Office, Adoption Section, Contact Register, Smedley Hydro, Trafalgar Road, Birkdale, Southport PR8 2HH

The registration fee should be sent with the completed application form. The Registrar General will return all birth and marriage certificates and other original personal documents to you after inspection. It is sometimes necessary for the Registrar General to ask for additional evidence to support an application.

If you change your mind about registration, you should write to the Registrar General asking him to remove your name and address from the Register. Twenty-eight-days' notice is required.

Please remember: while your name remains on the Register, it is important to let the Registrar General know if you change your address.

Using an address other than your own

18. The Adoption Contact Register has been set up to help adopted people and their birth parents and other relatives make contact. Some relatives of adopted people may want to register an address other than their own because they may not want to be contacted direct. That is why the Registrar General is able to register an address 'through which contact can be made' as an alternative to a relative's home address. An alternative address supplied should be that of an organisation or individual such as a social worker or counsellor who has agreed to act as an inter-mediary. Any relative who would prefer to learn of a Register link through a third person, with support available if needed, can consider using the address of such an intermediary. If you are happy to register your own address, the adopted person can choose to approach you direct.

When a register link occurs

19. An adopted person will receive the name and address supplied by the relative which may be either the relative's own address or that of an intermediary. A relative will be advised that information about him/her has been sent to the adopted person. It will then be up to the adopted person to act on the information. However, deciding at this stage to take no action, even through a third party, may cause disappointment and is not the purpose of the Register.

20. An adopted person who received a relative's home address should act sensitively and with care. It may be tempting to telephone a relative or just turn up at his or her home. This may not be a good idea as the adopted person will have no knowledge of the relative's circumstances. Discussion with a counsellor can help as he or she will be able to suggest helpful ways of proceeding.

21. There may be disappointment at first if a relative has supplied an address which is not his or her own. It should not be assumed that this has been done to avoid anyone. He or she may feel a need for support in establishing contact. Using an intermediary is a way of ensuring that help is at hand. An intermediary will try to help obtain the information which is most important

and his or her experience in acting as a 'go-between' in these circumstances can be very useful.

After receiving the notification of the link, you may wish to consider consulting an experienced counsellor who will be able to advise you how to go about contacting your relative.

Organisations providing advice and counselling

22. All local authority Social Services Departments provide counselling for people who have any problems concerning adoption: this includes adopted people, birth parents and adoptive parents. You should contact your Social Services Department for details of services available.

Voluntary adoption societies provide counselling in connection with adoptions they have arranged. If you are involved with an adoption arranged by an adoption society you can contact the society for discussion and advice. This applies whether you are an adopted person, a birth parent or an adoptive parent.

23. All completed Application Forms should be returned to:
Office for National Statistics
The General Register Office
Adoption Section, Contact Register
Smedley Hydro, Trafalgar Road
Birkdale, Southport PR8 2HH

© Department of Health and ONS
September 1998

What is the Adoption Information Line?

The Adoption Information Line and its sister service The Fostering Information Line assist local authority social services departments and adoption agencies to recruit carers for the children they have identified as being in need of foster care or adoption placements.

We provide information and advice to members of the general public on all aspects of fostering and adoption. Even if you have only just started to think about adoption you can call to ask any questions you might have. Then you can think about it some more and if you decide you want to pursue the idea further contact us again.

We also help other organisations in this field to develop information about what they do for the internet. For instance we have helped the British Agencies for Adoption and Fostering (BAAF) develop their web site which lists many of their publications, training events and membership details.

Our organisation has a Freephone line on 0800 783 4086.

It is open from 9am to 9pm, seven days a week, excluding Bank Holidays.

Our trained helpline staff provide on-the-spot friendly advice to people considering adoption. We are here to help so don't feel reluctant in any way to call us.

If we are requested to do so, we can put enquirers in touch with social services departments or other adoption agencies who are seeking foster carers or adopters in their area.

We also provide up-to-date information on the internet concerning a host of adoption and foster care topics. If you want to see a topic covered on our site please let us know.

On some of our pages we feature young people who are currently needing adoption placements. The photographs of children we use are of models and not of the actual children featured.

Our two internet site addresses are:
http://www.adoption.org.uk
and
http://www.fostering.org.uk

Our expertise in advertising, multimedia, graphic design and recruitment issues can be made available to social workers and their managers upon request. Simply give us a call to find out what we can do.

• The above information is from the Adoption and Fostering Information Line (AFIL) web site. See page 41 for their postal address details.

© Adoption and Fostering Information Line (AFIL)

Disabled people adopting children

Being disabled should not automatically exclude anyone from becoming an adopter. Often disabled people can provide a very loving home for a child that will meet their needs just as well as able-bodied adopters.

We often receive phone calls from disabled people who are very anxious about applying to become an adopter. Our advice is that you should contact us or your local social services department to get as much written information on adoption as you can. You should also try to attend any introductory sessions on adoption that are being held in your area. The fact that a person is disabled is only one of the issues that needs to be considered by the adoption agency, if and when you decide to apply to adopt, and should not be an issue for them before that time.

If such an approach is taken you will be able to gather lots of information upon which to base your decision to apply. One of the factors you will need time to consider is how your disability might affect your ability to provide for a child both now and in the future.

Many social services departments are seeking to improve their assessment techniques in relation to adoption applications from disabled people but it will always prove helpful if you have spent time considering what, if any, impact your disability might have upon you performing the task of caring for a young person.

Even if you believe that you might need some additional assistance to adopt a young person the onus should be upon the social services department to show that this assistance is not practical for them to perform and not necessarily upon you to demonstrate how you can work around any difficulties you might have.

Individual social workers do not deal with many applications from disabled people and you may find that both of you have quite a bit to learn during the assessment and adoption training process.

Many social workers working with children will not have a very good knowledge of disability which makes clarity essential. For example, if you have a disabling illness that is progressive you will know much more about the likely progress and impact of the illness. Try to make sure that you pass this knowledge on to the social worker. This will help to avoid them making assumptions about your progressive condition that may be incorrect.

Despite these problems you should always consider that, as with all would-be adopters, what you have to offer is special and would be suitable for certain children.

Clearly there are some levels of disability which would make it very difficult for you to be considered as an applicant to adopt. This decision should be made on an individual basis and against a background of a thorough knowledge of your disability and the impact it has or will have in the future upon you and your ability to care for a young person.

The Adoption Information Line wishes to promote the adoption of children. We believe that the disabled and the able bodied all have a contribution to make. If you are disabled and experience difficulties, or feel that you are being unfairly treated in relation to an application to adopt, please let us know. With your help we can work towards changing attitudes and improving the way in which applications from disabled people are treated.

Adopting a disabled child

Children with disabilities ranging from babies to teenagers may be placed for adoption. Sometimes their birth parents may feel unable to care for them or they may be placed for adoption for reasons which are not connected with their disability.

Some of these children have learning difficulties such as those with Down's syndrome whilst others may have been physically disabled from birth or suffered an accident or injury that has resulted in them being disabled.

In 1998 the Department of Health found that within every 100,00 of the population the incidence of some of these disabilities were:

- with a mild learning difficulty – 2,000
- with a moderate / severe learning difficulty – 300-400
- with significant challenging behaviour – 115-360
- with additional mental health problems – 115-1,200
- with impaired hearing – 920-960
- with epilepsy – 230-260
- with cerebral palsy – 230-260

This tells us that children with such disabilities are not a rarity both within the general population and amongst the children for whom adoption placements are being sought.

Whatever a child's disability they, like all other children, need the love and security that family life can offer. Disabled children are capable of offering a great deal of

love and affection in return and are just as rewarding to their carers as a child without disabilities.

Many disabled children will be able to lead independent or semi-independent lives when they are older whilst some others will continue to need to be cared for throughout their lives. One of the issues which you will want to think about and consider with their social worker is how the child may be supported over the long term.

Adopters of disabled children need understanding and commitment but they do not have to be 'very special people'. We hear from those who adopt disabled children just how 'ordinary' they are. 'We don't have any special powers or abilities. We just love children and our adopted youngster just gives us so much more love in return.'

We believe that many more adopters are capable of providing a happy, stable and supportive family to a disabled child than is generally recognised. Even the propective adopters themselves may not think of considering adopting a disabled child.

All adoption agencies approve both single adopters and couples, with children and without children, to adopt disabled children. They can give financial assistance in the form of adoption and other allowances to those who decide to adopt a disabled child.

• For further details please call us on the freephone line: 0800 783 4086. Or see page 41 for our address details.

Take adoption away from local authorities says report

Adoption should be taken away from local authority social services departments and handed over to voluntary organisations, according to a new report from the Institute of Economic Affairs. Adoptions fell from 21,000 in 1975 to under 6,000 in 1995, with baby adoptions down over the period from four-and-a-half thousand to a negligible 322. This is in spite of the fact that adopted children usually thrive, whereas children left in the local authority care system are unlikely to do well.

Political correctness clouds the judgement of childcare professionals

In *Adoption and the Care of Children: The British and American Experience* Patricia Morgan argues that the prejudice against adoption among childcare professionals is so great that – whilst claiming to be in favour of it in principle – they will find a reason to disqualify many applicants.

Prospective adoptive parents can be discouraged or ruled out on a variety of grounds, perhaps because they are too middle-class or because they have not had sufficient experience of racial prejudice! Children whose natural parents cannot or will not look after them properly are denied the options of a new adoptive home by social workers who insist that every effort must be made to reunite the original family. This can result in years of shuttling the child back and forth between council care, foster parents and the original parents, who may continue to abuse or neglect the child. If the child is ever made available for adoption he or she may have been so traumatised by this regime as to be extremely difficult to adopt.

Misguided enforcement of 'parental rights'

Patricia Morgan identifies this emphasis on the absolute rights of biological parents – misnamed 'family preservation' – which pervades childcare legislation and practice, as the most potent current mechanism for obstructing adoption. The most hopeless and even abusive parents are given limitless time and resources, with no limits or targets ever set, so that they can effectively blight their child's development without ever having to accept responsibility. Although legislation is in place to allow children to be declared free for adoption even if the birth-parents oppose it, this is seldom used.

This prolonged state of uncertainty and impermanence, which has damaging consequences for the child, is frequently justified by social workers as a requirement of the Children Act 1989 which is supposed to have advocated 'partnership with parents' – a phrase which does not occur in the Act. According to Patricia Morgan: 'It is better to face the possibility of conflict, than to sacrifice the child. If parents do not co-operate there must be a confrontation and, if necessary, legal action must be taken to free the child for adoption.'

Trans-racial adoptions are usually successful

Of all the justifications now used for blocking adoption, none is more controversial than the opposition to 'trans-racial adoption'. This means adoption by parents of one race (usually white) of a child of another race or mixed race. Trans-racial adoption, according to the accepted wisdom among social workers, destroys the child's sense of identity, causes confusion, and deprives the child of the mechanisms needed to cope with racism in society.

There is, in fact, no research evidence to support the claim that trans-racial adoption harms children in this way. Most trans-racial adoptions, like other adoptions, are successful. Furthermore, 'trans-racially adopted children actually had a much more accurate and positive perception of their race than other

black children. At the same time, they were more indifferent to race as a basis for evaluation than any other group.'

There is a mis-match between large numbers of black and mixed-race children who are in need of new homes, and small numbers of prospective black adoptive parents. The insistence upon matching racial profiles means that many of these children will stay in care for years, and possibly for their whole childhoods.

The consequences

One black boy had been fostered by a white couple for 14 years. Wanting security, he asked the local social services if the family could adopt him. The social workers then set about finding him a black home. According to a member of the foster panel concerned: 'the suggested adoptive black family lived in homeless accommodation, the father had convictions for violence. They were supposed to be the best of three – I don't know what the other two were like, I didn't like to ask.'

Adoption has excellent outcomes

The unwillingness to use adoption as a strategy for children who, for whatever reason, cannot live with their birth-parents, is hard to explain in view of the excellent outcomes associated with it. Adopted children do very well by all measures. Some studies show that they do as well as, or almost as well as, children brought up by both biological parents. But, as Patricia Morgan argues, this is not the right comparison to make.

Children who are adopted should be compared not with children in stable two-parent families – as that is not an option for them – but with children who grow up in the care of the local authority, which would be the alternative to adoption.

Children in local authority care often 'graduate' to unemployment, homelessness and crime

The outcomes for children in care, whether in children's homes or foster-care or – most likely – in a never-ending series of placements involving multiple disruptions to the child's life, are extremely poor. They are highly likely to 'graduate' from the care system to homelessness, unemployment and crime:

- a quarter of adult prisoners and 38% of young prisoners were in local authority care before the age of 16;
- ex-care children are four times more likely to be unemployed than other young people aged 16-24;
- they are 60 times more likely to be homeless;
- they are 50 times more likely to be imprisoned.

Some studies show that adopted children do as well as, or almost as well as, children brought up by both biological parents

We now know that the state makes a very bad substitute parent.

Breaking the deadlock

Patricia Morgan proposes a series of measures to break the deadlock which is blighting the lives of thousands of children whose parents are unwilling or unable to look after them:

- if parents whose children have been taken into care are not fit to have their children back at the end of 12 months, then procedures to free the child for adoption should be instigated. In exceptional circumstances the period could be extended to 24 months;
- any child left voluntarily in care for six months should be treated as abandoned and similarly made available for adoption;
- local authorities should be required to publish details of the number of children in their care and how long they have been there;
- adoption should be removed from local authority social services departments and vested in voluntary bodies who are genuinely committed to finding good adoptive homes for children in need of them.

• *Adoption and the Care of Children: The British and American Experience*, by Patricia Morgan, is published by the IEA Health and Welfare Unit, 2 Lord North Street, London SW1P 3LB, Tel 0171 799 3745, price £10 inc. p+p.
© The Institute of Economic Affairs (IEA) March, 1998

Adoption procedure 'is failing children'

By Philip Johnston, Home Affairs Editor

Britain's adoption system is a 'politically-correct lottery' in need of reform if thousands of children in care are to be found a home, campaigners claim today.

At the start of National Adoption Week, ministers are being urged to set up a central authority to oversee the decisions of social workers and other agencies. It would also monitor the operation of adoptions between countries.

Although there are more than 40,000 children in care or with foster parents, only 2,300 are found new families each year. Overall, the number of adoptions has fallen from 21,000 in 1975 to below 6,000. Adoptions of babies have fallen from 4,500 to 322.

The British Agencies for Adoption and Fostering, which is organising the campaign week, says that 10,000 children need new families.

The Adoption Forum, an independent think-tank, says: 'The present arrangements are failing at great cost to prospective adopters and most of all to children, many of whom linger in local authority care far longer than is in their best interest.

'Common sense and pragmatism frequently take second place to an over-zealous application of theory to everyday situations and the concerns of politically-correct decision-making.'

A study published this year found that an in-built hostility to mixed-race adoptions was partly to blame for the shortfall in prospective parents.

New guidelines were published in the summer by the health minister, Paul Boateng, ending the automatic exclusion of mixed-race or middle-class families.

'It is unacceptable for a child to be denied loving adoptive parents solely on the grounds that the child and adopters do not share the same racial or cultural background,' he said.

But campaigners fear the guidelines will make little difference. Similar rules were issued in 1990 and yet local authorities – taking their lead from the Children Act – continued to block adoptions for a variety of reasons ranging from the colour of the parents to the fact that one or both smoked.

> *Overall, the number of adoptions has fallen from 21,000 in 1975 to below 6,000. Adoptions of babies have fallen from 4,500 to 322*

While not all children in care are suitable for adoption, there is a body of evidence showing that many who spend their childhood in local authority homes have a life of under-achievement.

Apart from the abuse scandals that have surrounded some residential homes, children leaving care are four times more likely than others to be unemployed and 60 times more likely to be homeless. A quarter of adults in prison were in care at the age of 16.

A paper published today by the Adoption Forum and the Campaign of Inter-Country Adoption says local authorities and other agencies will remain resistant to change unless they are pressed into action by a central authority.

The proposed authority would oversee the actions of social workers and license voluntary agencies. It would have the power to withdraw licences from agencies that failed to meet national criteria and to suspend individual social workers.

It would also keep a national register of approved adopters and act as the central agency for inter-country adoptions.

Liv O'Hanlon, director of the Adoption Forum, said they did not propose taking adoptions out of the hands of local authorities but believed they should be made more accountable.

'Anti-adoption culture' to be investigated

By Andrew Grice,
Political Editor

The watchdog body for local authorities is set to investigate criticism that councils are reluctant to allow children in care to be adopted.

The Audit Commission said yesterday that an inquiry into adoption was being considered following requests from MPs. David Davis, chairman of the Commons Public Accounts Committee, wrote to the commission after *The Independent* revealed that ministers plan to act over the 'anti-adoption culture' of Britain's social workers.

Mr Davis asked Andrew Foster, the commission's controller, to probe the 'dreadfully poor results of keeping children in care, and the enormous variation in the levels of adoption in different authorities'. Local authorities spend £2.25bn a year on services for children. Although 50,000 are in their care, the number of adoptions has fallen from 21,000 in the seventies to just 2,000 a year.

'This issue has huge implications for social services costs, and even greater consequences for the lives of the children involved,' said Mr Davis, Conservative MP for Haltemprice and Howden. He said an urgent investigation by the commission into local authority practices would be extremely valuable and underpin future government action and policy.

Mr Davis welcomed the decision by a cabinet committee on the family, chaired by Jack Straw, the Home Secretary, to launch a review of the adoption laws. Mr Davis believes social workers use existing rules, saying that children should be reunited with their natural parents where possible, as an excuse to avoid adoptions, even though there is often little prospect of them returning home.

> '*There is a large pool of children who would benefit from being adopted, while the taxpayer would benefit from a considerable cost saving*'

Julian Brazier, organiser of an all-party group of MPs which supports adoption, told the commission that 24,000 of the 50,000 children being 'looked after' by local authorities had been in care for at least two years.

Most natural parents who took children back from care successfully did so within six months; very few young people returned home if they had been in care for more than 18 months.

'There is a large pool of children who would benefit from being adopted, while the taxpayer would benefit from a considerable cost saving,' he said.

Mr Brazier said young people leaving care were 50 times more likely than other children to go to prison; those who had been in care made up 38 per cent of young offenders and 23 per cent of adult prisoners.

'Youth crime currently costs £1bn per annum, and it can clearly be seen that the care system accounts for a substantial proportion of it,' said Mr Brazier.

Last night Mr Brazier welcomed the cabinet's initiative and said his all-party group would keep up the pressure on ministers to bring in a new Adoption Act before the next general election. 'This is not about party politics,' said Mr Brazier, Tory MP for Canterbury. 'The top priority is the welfare of the children. The best place for a child to grow up is in a caring, loving family.'

© *The Independent*
March, 1999

Councils named in adoption crisis

By Andrew Grice,
Political Editor

New evidence that local authorities are refusing to allow thousands of children in care to be adopted has emerged in a nation-wide survey by House of Commons officials.

Some councils with hundreds of young people in their care permit only a handful of adoptions each year, according to the figures. Several Labour-run London boroughs are among those with the lowest rates of finding permanent new families for problem children.

Until now, pro-adoption pressure groups could not find out how many of the 51,000 children in care were being adopted in each area, but the number being placed has dropped from 21,000 a year in the Seventies to 2,000. The first detailed breakdown was compiled by researchers in the Commons library.

The statistics have fuelled allegations that the 'anti-adoption culture' of social workers is condemning young people to grow up in council-run homes. *The Independent* revealed last month that the Government intended to crack down on authorities who were dragging their feet. The figures foreshadow a 'league table' being compiled by the Department of Health.

The Commons survey revealed that the number of adoptions in England dropped from 2,500 in 1993 to 1,900 in 1997. The London borough of Ealing had the lowest rate in 1997, when just one of the 393 children in its care was adopted. In the previous two years, Ealing permitted 12 and 8 adoptions respectively.

Ten councils approved the adoption of just 1 per cent of the children they 'looked after' in 1997 (see table, plus Hillingdon with three). Another 21 authorities approved the adoption of 2 per cent. They were Greenwich (six children); Hammersmith and Fulham (five); Lambeth (13); Southwark (14); Hounslow (six); Wandsworth (nine); Stockton on Tees (four children); Manchester (26); Salford (seven); Liverpool (20); Sefton (five); North Yorkshire (six); Calderdale (six); Hereford and Worcester (12); Shropshire (six); Sandwell (nine); Devon (20); Somerset (nine); Suffolk (13); Oxfordshire (eight); Surrey (16).

At the other end of the scale, the authorities with the highest percentage of adoptions were Hartlepool, North Lincolnshire and York, which found permanent new homes for 10 per cent of their children.

Julian Brazier, who is the founder of an informal group of pro-adoption MPs, and who commissioned the survey, said the figures were shocking. He was alarmed that London authorities whose running of children's homes had been criticised were among those reluctant to permit adoptions. He hoped that councillors in the areas with low adoption rates would now 'sit up and take notice' of the figures. 'Children's lives are being blighted as they are moved from one council home to another or one temporary foster parent to another,' he said.

Mr Brazier, Tory MP for Canterbury, urged the Government to punish at least one council by closing its adoption service and handing responsibility to a neighbouring authority or voluntary group. This would 'concentrate the minds' of other councils, he said.

Last night, local authority leaders admitted that the new figures showed some councils needed to take a more positive attitude towards adoption.

John Ransford, head of social affairs at the Local Government Association, said: 'Clearly there are signs that adoption is a course that should be considered more quickly, robustly and actively.'

But he insisted that some councils may have high numbers of difficult-to-place children, and their figures did not necessarily mean they were not trying to find adoptive families. 'Adoption is for life; you have got to be sure the match is exactly right for the child and for the family,' he said.

The worst authorities

Council	Children in care	Adoptions	% of children in care adopted
Ealing	393	1	0.25%
Hackney	466	3	0.6%
Bury	179	1	0.6%
Newcastle	408	3	0.7%
Hants	1,154	8	0.7%
Gloucestershire South	140	2	1.4%
Haringey	289	4	1.4%
North Tyneside	283	4	1.4%
Merton	173	2	1.2%
Brent	329	4	1.2%

Figures for 1997   *Source: House of Commons*

This adoption scandal

It's one of the social crimes of our age. Never have so many people wanted to adopt and so few children been adopted. Here, a leading writer uncovers a politically correct nightmare which is causing such bitter unhappiness for needy youngsters and would-be parents alike. Special investigation by David Jones

Living in a spacious, well-furbished home deep in the East Anglian countryside, a caring married couple want for nothing – except a child. Told they will never be able to conceive, they decide to adopt, and prepare themselves for months of rigorous inspection and re-inspection by social workers.

They are ready to answer the most personal questions imaginable…questions about previous relationships, their attitudes towards homosexuality, their racial and religious beliefs, and their own dimly remembered childhood experiences.

It is emotionally draining and, at times, humiliating. But then, 50,000 children are in care and there is a huge shortage of suitable adoptive parents. Surely they would be allowed to share their love with just one?

Even as they thumb through magazines which advertise children seeking a family, they are informed that the local adoption panel has rejected them as unsuitable.

The reason? 'The location of your home,' their case worker tells them flatly. 'It's far too isolated for the needs of a young child.'

As the shock subsides, the couple protest. They have a car and the nearest village is only a few minutes' drive away. It has a school, shops, a church. Besides, what better place to try to repair the damage of a broken home than in a peaceful corner of rural England? But their pleas fall on deaf ears.

Some might dismiss this case – only slightly modified to protect the identity of those involved – as unusual. In fact, set alongside the numerous stories related to me during a lengthy investigation into the nation's failing adoption system, it is depressingly typical.

So typical that Philippa Morrall, the national co-ordinator of Parent To Parent Information On Adoption Services, says: 'If you put them [the examples of blocked adoption applications] all together, you would think the world had turned upside down.'

Accepting the latest and best research, which indicates that adoption is broadly a good thing – in that it transforms neglected, mistreated or unwanted children into secure, well-adjusted adults – why, then, are the hopes of so many youngsters being thwarted?

Why, when the numbers in care are slowly rising, did the number of adoptions fall to just 1,900 for the year ending March 31, 1997 – a figure which is expected to alter little when the latest Government statistics are released next month? And one which compares with an annual 20,000-plus throughout the Seventies.

How can we have reached the stage where many local authorities are placing just 1 per cent of children in their care with adoptive parents each year, and where two, Ealing and Waltham Forest in Greater London, placed one solitary child each in a 12-month period, according to the Department of Health?

The short answer is that the entire adoption system is a shambles and in drastic need of an overhaul.

A minefield for prospective parent and needy child alike, it is, in the words of Right-wing academic Patricia Morgan – who recently conducted an extensive research on adoption for the Policy Studies Institute – 'run by people who are inefficient at doing something they are largely opposed to anyway'.

Most adoptions, she concludes, 'take place in spite of the system, not because of it'.

To understand fully why, we might start with some recent history.

During the permissive Sixties and Seventies, when contraception was not so widely practised and abortions were undertaken less readily, it was the boom in unwanted babies that sparked a sharp rise in adoptions.

But problems began with the dawning of the age of political correctness.

Taking their lead from a radical black movement in America, sociologists in Britain deemed it wrong for children to be placed with parents of a different ethnic background. Never mind that this often deprived them of a permanent family. It was, they decreed, unwise and perhaps even dangerous to 'deny them their roots'.

The other doctrine that emerged was that, almost regardless of their natural parents' inadequacies – drunkenness, drug addiction and inability to cope – children were invariably better off with them than with adopters, no matter how superior their parenting skills.

These twin planks of dogma, drilled into every aspiring social worker during basic training, continue to obstruct the pathway to adoption today.

Philippa Morrall cites cases where aspiring adopters have been turned down because they were 'too middle class'. Others are rejected as too working class, 'whatever that means', she sighs.

One source told me of a black child fostered, happily, for four years by a white family. But when they asked permission to adopt him they were deemed unacceptable, and parents of his own colour were sought.

Government minister Paul Boateng – himself married to a social worker – recently promised to increase and speed up the adoption process.

Yet when examining the system at work, it becomes clear that wholesale changes are needed, not only in philosophy but in basic custom and practice.

An experienced freelance adoption specialist in North London illustrates why by reciting the following fictitious, but all too typical, case . . .

Baby Peter's parents are chronic drug-abusers, and when he is just a few months old the social services are informed. They visit his flat, immediately recognise that he is not being adequately looked after and obtain an emergency care order.

However, clinging to the vain hope that, eventually, he may be reunited with his mother and father, they do not alert family placement workers (in the same department). Instead they put Peter in temporary foster care while his parents are sent to a rehabilitation clinic.

Three months – and about £25,000 in clinic fees – later, the couple have split and it starts to dawn on the social workers that Peter is never going home. A fact that has been obvious to others from the start.

Now, with lawyers (at up to £120 per hour and perhaps £4,000 in total) and the assistance of a guardian *ad litem* acting for the child (average case fees £3,000), they return to court to seek a permanent care order.

With the judicial backlog, in London this can take five or six months, but even if the order is granted the bewildering process is far from over.

Although the social services have presented a care plan to the court, citing adoption as the best option for Peter, he cannot be 'freed' by the local adoption panel until his case worker has appraised them of every last detail about him – down to his nickname.

They must do this by completing one key document, known as Form E. To a social worker who knows her case, it should pose little difficulty. Our freelance adoption worker reckons it can be finished, in most cases, in three or four days.

But quite often, she says, uncompleted forms lie in the case file for a year or more. 'It's a sandal and even after 20 years in the business it makes my blood boil.'

What, then, of Peter? By now he is a toddler, and he has been in care for more than 18 months. Yet it is only now, when he has formed close bonds with his foster family, that the process of finding him adoptive parents begins.

Advertisements are placed in magazines such as *Be My Parent*, phone calls are made, lists of prospective adopters checked, couples vetted and requested to present their own tax return-style document (Form F) – work which might have been started months before.

The longer Peter remains with his foster parents, the greater the pain and emotional damage when his bonds with them are broken.

Then there is the mounting cost.

Using their own recruited foster family, a local authority might pay £140 a week per child.

But increasingly foster parents are operating through agencies which charge £500-plus a week, including their own cut, of course. So Peter's foster fees alone could top £35,000.

The other big outlay is the so-called inter-agency fee. Where local authorities can't match a child with adoptive parents in their own area, they are required to pay the authority where his new family lives £17,000 to cover costs.

To many local authorities, particularly smaller ones and those which are spending most of their funds on what they regard as more pressing social services, this sum is seen as prohibitive. They simply can't, or won't, pay.

Thus, we have a ludicrous situation where one area of the country has a waiting-list of approved adopters and another, perhaps just a short drive away, has children to suit them. Both sides are ready and available for adoption – but they cannot be matched together.

There are two further ironies. First these cash-strapped authorities – usually deprived inner-city boroughs – are precisely the ones with higher numbers of children in need of long-term care.

Secondly, though it may appear expensive in the short term, in the long term adoption can be viewed as remarkably cheap. Children left to languish for years in care are many times more likely to turn to crime (33 per cent of prisoners have been in care). They are also less likely to earn qualifications and get jobs.

Add up the consequent outlay – police, court, jail, welfare benefits – and the £60,000-plus for Peter's adoption is a relative bargain.

Given that the system is radically in need of an overhaul, then, what measures are needed to change it?

The Government is said to be so concerned about the poor record of social services departments on adoptions that it has not ruled out removing their responsibility for them altogether.

If that happened, the bulk of adoptions might be handled by a new central agency, streamlining the entire process. According to Jim Richards, widely respected in the field for his adoption work with the Catholic Children's Society, there is urgent need for a revision of the 1976 Adoption Act.

This was largely devised with the needs of thousands of unwanted but healthy babies in mind – not the older, multi-racial, special-needs children who fill most foster homes today.

Among the changes Mr Richards wants is a set timetable for the instigation of adoption proceedings where there is a prolonged lack of contact between the birth parent and child.

Where, during care proceedings, local authorities have stated that they plan to have a child adopted, he believes the case workers should be required to report back to the court at six-monthly intervals on that child's progress.

A third positive step, he says, would be for the annual statistics to reveal how many children need to be adopted. At present they say only how many have been.

Ultimately, however, he says, social services departments will need to improve their efficiency and the old politically correct attitudes will have to change.

People argue that a child's place is with the birth family and, once you have adoption, that is severed for ever. I don't hold with that because it seems to me you are not looking at the child's individual needs. If the need is adoption, then you have to go for it.

'The research shows that London boroughs are the slowest in the country at finding adopters and that could be something to do with philosophical factors. The other thing is lack of expertise in adoption, and high turn-over among social workers.

'In some boroughs I know, a child may have three or four social workers in one year. You aren't going to get adoption out of that. There is no continuity or commitment.'

Yes, it's a grim picture, but we ought not forget that there is another side to the adoption story. It centres on the many hundreds of couples who, against the odds, still manage to weave through the minefield and create successful adoptive families.

There are some happy endings. The East Anglian couple went to a specialist agency, Parents For Children, and have now successfully adopted a brother and sister.

Karen Irving, head of Parents For Children, says: 'We get a number of people who have not found it easy to adopt through local authorities and agencies, yet they make wonderful adopters.'

And during my enquiries I spoke to Margaret Boutelle, a remarkable 54-year-old divorcee who confounded her local authority by adopting, through an outside agency, two children, one with cerebral palsy, the other with a mental handicap.

It was difficult to tell who was the happier with the arrangement – Mrs Boutelle or her children.

Adoptive parents such as Mrs Boutelle offer a lifeline for Britain's most needy children. Surely they shouldn't be turned away simply because they are too middle class, or because their home is too far away from the nearest town?

© *The Daily Mail*
April, 1999

Adoption row over teenage mothers

By Vikram Dodd

Jack Straw, the Home Secretary, was last night at the centre of a political storm after he said that more teenage mothers should surrender their children for adoption.

Mr Straw said that 'well-meaning, but misguided' social workers underestimated the difficulties teenage women face dealing with the financial and emotional demands of parenthood.

In a speech to a conference organised by the Family Policy Studies Centre, Mr Straw said: 'It is in no one's interests, not the mother's, not the child's, nor the prospective parents', to allow a situation to develop whereby a crisis point is reached in the baby's first year because the ability of the mother,

often a teenage mother, to cope has been misjudged by well-meaning but misguided people.'

The result was that too many babies were being taken into council care, which he described as a 'state of limbo', until they could be placed in a proper home or with foster parents or adopted.

The remarks provoked a furious reaction from organisations working with young mothers, who accused Mr Straw of ignoring the emotional trauma women suffer when they give up their child.

Ann Furedi, of the British

Pregnancy Advisory Service, which provides abortion advice and help, said: 'Adoption is an entirely inappropriate solution to the problem of teenage parenthood. Fewer than 100 newborn babies a year are handed over for adoption, not because of legal difficulties, but because of emotional difficulties a woman faces when she gives away the child that she has borne.'

The comments have left campaigners stunned because they come from a Government which has put single mothers at the centre of its family agenda. Both the Social Exclusion Unit and the Women's Unit, which co-ordinates policy across Whitehall affecting women, are looking at the issue.

'It is remarkable that a Government that casts itself as caring should suggest this as a solution for teenage girls,' said Ms Furedi. 'A public health campaign aimed at teenagers to promote the effectiveness and safety of the contraceptive pill would be a far more sensible measure.'

Felicity Collier, director of the British Agencies for Adoption and Fostering, said that over 70 per cent of children in local authority care were returned to their natural parents within 12 months. 'We need to encourage support for all mothers, whatever their situation.'

Mr Straw said he was surprised that in 1997 there were more than 3,500 children under two being looked after by local authorities, while couples wanting to adopt had to wait for years.

He said local councils should not put up 'unnecessary barriers' and that teenage mothers unable to care for their children should be encouraged to see adoption as a 'positive, responsible choice'.

Mr Straw said: 'It is still a sad fact that many suitable couples have been on waiting lists far too long, while children have remained in care.'

Mr Straw said teenage mothers offering their children for adoption could result in a better life for the baby, though his speech avoided advocating a policy of forcing teenage single mothers to give their babies away: 'If you get to a situation where young mothers feel happy about adoption that's so much the better.

'It is better if these adoptions are done voluntarily than if the children are later taken into care.

'The Home Secretary said the Government had issued new guidelines to make adoption easier, but more work needed to be done to match up would-be parents and children.

He added that it had become fashionable to move away from adoption, and cited figures showing the number had dropped from 25,000 adoptions in 1968 to 6,000 a year.
• First published in *The Guardian*, January, 1999.   © *Vikram Dodd*

Adoption

Is Jack Straw right to say that unmarried teenagers should give their babies away?

Yes says Melanie Phillips

Jack Straw is absolutely right. In saying that more teenage mothers should be encouraged to give up their babies for adoption, he was speaking pure common sense. His comments are extremely significant. For the first time, a senior politician has made an unequivocal statement that puts the interests of vulnerable children first.

We know that lone parenthood is in general very bad for children, and isn't very good for the mothers, either. We know that teenage lone motherhood is little short of a disaster.

Children brought up in such circumstances do worse in virtually every area of their lives than children brought up by two committed parents. And we know that adoptive children do extremely well, overwhelmingly growing up to be well-adjusted individuals.

Yet pregnant girls are generally not even presented with adoption as an option when they visit their GP or family planning clinic. They are given two choices: muddle through on your own with the baby, or have an abortion.

No one talks to them about the advantages to the child of adoption.

No one thinks about the child, only about the mother. It's unnatural to give your baby away, goes the thinking, but natural to have it killed.

All those people who are so concerned for the feelings of the mother whose child is adopted are strangely silent about the lasting grief of the mother who has her baby aborted. Silent also about the damage done to children who languish in care.

As Jack Straw said, it is far better for children to be brought up by adoptive families than by the state. He is not saying mothers should be forced to have their babies adopted. He is merely saying that the babies of mothers who can't look after them properly should not be left in limbo in children's homes, or shunted between one temporary foster home

> *Children brought up in such circumstances do worse in virtually every area of their lives than children brought up by two committed parents*

and another, where they become more and more damaged.

Such mothers should be encouraged to place them instead in stable, loving families and give them secure identities.

Critics say that more than 70 per cent of children in care are returned to their natural families within a year. That leaves a sizeable 30 per cent who are not. And of those who do return, how many go back into neglectful or abusive homes from which they have to be rescued and returned into care?

Social workers prefer fostering to adoption because it enables them to keep control over families. This is why for years now the rate of adoptions has been falling, while fostering has increased. And that's why often indefensible obstacles are placed in the way of couples desperate to adopt.

Social workers protest that they aren't blocking adoptions. But the game has been given away by Moira Gibb, vice-president of the Association Of Social Services Directors, who said society didn't want to see babies 'farmed out to middle-class mothers'.

What on earth has class got to

do with it? Does she think only middle-class people are childless? Many adoptive parents are people of modest means. Her remarks appear to reflect the poisonous ideological attitude which says, falsely, that the traditional nuclear family of two parents bringing up children is middle class and somehow alien to everyone else. But it's what every child wants or, if deprived of it, dreams of having.

Much has been made of the pain of mothers giving up their children for adoption. No one would deny this is traumatic and deeply distressing. But what about the harm or distress caused to children in care, or those left in abusive or neglectful homes because the interests of their natural mothers are always put first?

A mother who brings a child into the world when she cannot look after it practically, emotionally or financially forfeits her 'right' to have it. Parents don't have rights over their children but duties towards them. And real love always means acting in the child's best interests.

The visceral opposition to Straw's comments derives from the pernicious view that a child is owned by its mother, to be disposed of or dealt with solely in accordance with her own feelings and desires.

Teenage pregnancy is complex and there is no single solution. But the message has to be got across that getting pregnant irresponsibly and expecting someone else to pick up the tab just isn't on any more – for teenagers or anyone else.

Straw has shown considerable courage in opening up this vital issue. He now faces a vile onslaught as a result.
• Melanie Phillips is a columnist on the *Sunday Times*.

No says Angela Neustatter

One can't help wondering if Jack Straw stopped for even a moment to consider how he would have felt if he had been 'persuaded' to give up his own child for adoption. Or how his child would have felt knowing that he had been given up by his natural parents.

Did this even cross his mind before he came up with his solve-the-difficulty-at-one-stroke solution

to the 'problem' of teenage mothers and, with it, the unhappiness of 'suitable' families who are thwarted in their desire to adopt a baby because feckless, wilful young mothers insist on keeping them.

For the most startling thing about the Home Secretary's speech to the Family Policy Studies con-ference on Monday was that it seemed to be more about cutting government spending than concern for the welfare of the child or the mother.

In one easy move, he could get benefit cuts and make supplies of children available to self-supporting families. Now that's the kind of imaginative thinking we expect from a Labour government.

But there is the human price to be considered too. The stories of lifelong anguish told by women who have given up children for adoption are harrowing. So, too, are the stories of those who carry with them the permanent scars of rejection because they were given up as babies.

Adopted children can suffer a very real loss of identity as a result of their 'abandonment' which, in adulthood, may jeopardise their own chances of forming lasting relation-ships.

I recall the experience of a woman friend who was adopted and who eventually found the hospital where she was born.

Reading the notes, she saw the phrase: 'Her mother refused to pick her up.' You and I might be able to understand that this mother could not bear the pain of bonding with the child who would be taken from her. But, for my friend, it has never stopped meaning that she was not lovable.

Of course, it is not ideal that single teenagers have children. But nor are all these young mums necessarily so 'unsuitable' that social workers should effectively be given

---

The truth is that a good many teenage women whose pregnancies are unplanned nevertheless go on to be remarkably good mothers

---

carte blanche, as Jack Straw suggests, to persuade them they will not be able to cope.

Straw seems to have accepted the Right-wing dogma that un-married teenage mothers are, by definition, irresponsible and hopeless, and incapable of parenting their children adequately. They are not individuals – the good, the bad and the mediocre, like all the rest of us parents – but a homogeneous group who are simply using the children they bear to acquire council flats and easy money.

The truth is that a good many teenage women whose pregnancies are unplanned nevertheless go on to be remarkably good mothers.

I know this partly from my own work interviewing teenage mothers. I have found myself startled by the healthy, happy and well-adjusted children I have come across living with mothers. These women could not have been more devoted or self-sacrificing in their desire to bring up their child well.

It is wrong to assume that class defines good parenting. How dare anyone say that a middle-class adoptive mother is a far better option for a young child than a teenager in reduced circumstances.

Right-wing propagandists find it difficult to accept that couples who adopt may often lack vital parenting qualities. They are often so desperate for a child that they are unrealistic in their expectations of what a son or daughter may bring to their lives. Then they are disappointed if the child fails to deliver. It is not unheard of for adoptive parents to return children to social services.

I know the standard argument that providing teenage mothers with support to help them cope only encourages them to have babies. It is an argument that is not supported by evidence.

But when we punish teenage mothers, we also punish the innocent children. No bond is stronger than the blood bond. It not only creates enormous love but often an under-standing of the child that an adoptive parent may not have.
• First published in the *Daily Mail*, January, 1999.
© *Melanie Phillips/Angela Neustatter*

Couples barred from adopting children of a single mother

Social workers are preventing children abandoned by single mothers from being adopted by couples, it has emerged.

They insist that the vulnerable youngsters go to homes with single parents, according to the country's biggest adoption agency, which apparently backs the trend.

Social workers believe having two parents will unsettle children who have only lived with one, says the independent British Agencies for Adoption and Fostering in its newspaper *Be My Parent* – aimed at those who want to adopt.

Children with one parent were now 'steered' towards adoption by another single parent because that 'will feel familiar and less disruptive'.

The trend will put a fresh barrier between children desperately needing homes and the middle-class married couples queueing up to take them.

It was condemned by MPs concerned with adoption, who insisted that married couples provide the best chance of a good start in life for thousands of children caught in the state care system.

Last week the *Daily Mail* revealed how large numbers of youngsters living in foster or council homes are denied the chance of adoption by a loving family because of the ideology of social workers who block adoptions on grounds of race or age.

Now some social workers in favour of single parents appear to be denying abandoned children the chance of a stable life with two married parents.

The BAAF declares: 'Social workers, wherever possible, try to replicate the family structure the child has come from.

'For those children who have grown up in lone parent households (estimated at one in five) moving to a new life with a single carer will feel familiar and less disruptive.'

By Steve Doughty, Social Affairs Correspondent

The BAAF had 'expressed anger' at moves by MPs to give married couples preference in adoption because that would mean the 'needs of looked-after children' would be 'sacrificed because of a preconceived notion of what constitutes a family'.

The article goes on: 'Not only do many adopted children thrive with a single parent, they are the first family of choice for some.'

The claim that social workers are blocking two-parent adoption for children of single mothers was greeted with alarm by MPs and family campaigners.

Julian Brazier, Tory MP for Canterbury and head of a group of senior backbenchers pressing ministers for change in adoption regulations, said: 'No objective study has ever supported what the BAAF is saying.

'It flies in the face of all the evidence, which shows that children do best when they have two married parents.'

Hugh McKinney, of the Conservative Family Campaign, commented: 'Every single piece of research over the last 30 years has shown that children brought up by married couples do better than others.

'It is outrageous to suggest single parents are better because a child was born to a single mother.

'It puts in place a new prejudice against married couples and a barrier to stop adoption by the people children in care need most.'

Home Secretary Jack Straw has been pressing for social workers to pay more attention to adoption in the face of figures showing many children spend years trapped in the care system instead of having families found for them.

He has blamed 'unprofessional' social workers for much of the problem.

BAAF director Felicity Collier last night backtracked on the article in her organisation's newspaper. She said the claim that social workers try to replicate a child's family was incorrect and that they 'always assess the individual needs of each child before deciding what family situation would be best'.

Miss Collier added that single adopters 'provide a valuable resource for children given the positive messages in our research about the success of single parent adoptions'.

© *The Daily Mail*
March, 1999

Adoption by single people

Unique research claims single parents can make excellent adoptive parents

'I just wanted someone mature and agreeable, someone who lived on a quiet street with bumpy roads for my BMX bike – and I found her!'

A unique study published this week by the British Agencies for Adoption and Fostering (BAAF) describes the experiences of 30 single adults who have adopted and 48 of the children placed with them. *Novices, Old Hands & Professionals, Adoption by Single People*, a study by Morag Owen, is the first research to look in detail at this sensitive area of practice and draw conclusions for policy makers. The text is full of moving and important quotes from the adoptive parents and their children. The study concludes that single adopters are an undervalued and underused resource, that they have special skills and commitment which can provide unique opportunities to children awaiting adoption and that children raised by a single carer do not generally feel disadvantaged by having one parent.

Key findings:

- Though the single adopters had widely varied backgrounds, interests and experiences they also had certain qualities in common. They were all extremely committed to adoption and were confident in their ability to form a positive relationship with a child. They included novices (people with no previous experience of bringing up children), old hands (old carers who wanted to use the skills they had acquired in raising their own children) and professionals (single people with work experience directly related to adoption who wished to form a one-to-one relationship with a child).
- Social stigma deterred many of the adopters from applying

Information from the British Agencies for Adoption and Fostering (BAAF)

sooner. Some had felt that they would not be accepted because of their marital status and others believed that adoption regulations are more rigid than is actually the case.

- Single people were sometimes not considered as adopters for a child until the search to find a couple had proved fruitless. Single men were considered less eligible than single women.

The children

- All the children placed with the single people in the study were classified as having special needs. Their average age was between four and five years old. 22 were older white children, many of whom had a background of abuse or neglect, 16 were black or of mixed parentage needing culturally specific placements, and 10 were physically or mentally disabled. Nearly half the children had learning difficulties.
- Most children felt that there was no particular disadvantage associated with having one parent and they did not feel themselves to be significantly different from other children who had two parents. A few children counted it as an actual advantage to have one parent because it made life simple and conflict-free.
- Girls who had been sexually abused said that they found the experience of living with a single mother a healing and sheltering one.
- The quality of the relationship between the children and the adoptive parent was, on the whole, extremely good. 87% of the children in the 10–15 age

group said they got along with their adoptive parents 'very well'.

- The experiences of black single adopters and children were different from those of white adopters and children. They felt that they had to overcome more hurdles throughout the adoption process.

Felicity Collier, Director, BAAF: 'This book confirms what families and social workers have long known – that single adopters can provide vulnerable children with stable and loving homes but may be unaware that they are eligible to be adopters. It is very impressive that after several years all the adoptions reported in this study were working out and none of the children had returned to care. This is a remarkable achievement for children with such diverse needs.

'This is a welcome success story at a time when there has been much public concern about the children of single parents. There is a shortage of adoptive parents for children who have particular needs, often relating to their age and previous experiences, and we know that many of them wait far too long. The lack of encouragement experienced by single adopters and the discrimination some of them say they have faced is saddening as this may stop suitable people from applying and could undermine their confidence in their parenting skills. It is clear that agencies need to improve information and ease of access if the skills of single people are to be used in adoption. Single people are potentially a flexible as well as talented resource for waiting children.'

• *Novices, Old Hands & Professionals, Adoption by Single People* is available from BAAF. Price £11.95. See page 41 for address details.

© British Agencies for Adoption and Fostering (BAAF) February, 1999

One parent is enough

Marriage 'no longer important for families wanting to adopt children'

Social workers have been told they need no longer give priority to married couples when choosing volunteers to adopt children.

The move means single people, including lone parents, are considered equally and raises the spectre of homosexuals finding it much easier to adopt.

The switch, pushed through in new guidelines to social services directors, means the Government has caved in to years of pressure from social workers and adoption agencies and undermined its pledge to support the institution of marriage. Yesterday it brought criticism from experts who warned that inviting some single people to adopt would lower the standard of homes for adopted children.

For the past three years, the guidelines have clearly favoured married couples for adoption.

They stated: 'Most children in the UK are brought up within a family comprising a father and a mother whose relationship and commitment are recognised in marriage and who

By Steve Doughty, Social Affairs Correspondent

have legal responsibilities to each other. There is a presumption that for most children, such a structure offers the best chance for successful development into adulthood through a stable and enduring relationship with two parents.'

The 1996 rules also warned that 'careful attention' had to be paid to aspects of adoptions by single people, including the possible presence of other adults.

But all mention of marriage has been omitted from new guidelines from the Department of Health. Instead, they stress the importance to a child of 'membership of a permanent family' but no longer specify the kind of family.

Social workers are also warned against delaying adoptions on race grounds. The Department of Health said: 'We have to place a child with the best person available. If that is a

single person then they can be chosen as well as a married couple.' The change is likely to lead to a wave of adoptions by single people with incalculable effects on the children, sociologist Patricia Morgan warned yesterday. 'It enshrines in the rules the idea that all families are the same, which patently they are not,' she said.

Mrs Morgan, who writes on adoption for the Institute for Economic Affairs, also claimed it would make same-race placements easier because there are many black single parents wishing to adopt, but a comparative shortage of black married couples.

At present adoption by single people is rare – and usually involves a woman unlikely to find a new partner taking on a child who had been sexually abused. But a report from the British Agencies for Adoption and Fostering described single adopters as 'undervalued and underused'.

© The Daily Mail February, 1999

Secrets, lies and the burning need to discuss adoption

By Yasmin Alibhai-Brown

Adoption is a hot issue. Hot enough to be untouchable most of the time. Part of the problem is that there are so many fundamentalists involved in the business and they will die fighting for the right not to question or change the way things are done. Many a strong beast has been cowed by the ferocity of this self-righteousness. The contentious or courageous (depending on your point of view) Jack Straw has just been forced to confront these soldiers for daring to suggest that teenage mothers could be encouraged to consider adoption

as a real option when they have their babies.

Speaking at the Family Policy Studies Centre, Straw said, I think quite rationally, that there are, at present, 3,500 small children in care and part of the problem is that professionals dealing in this area are too obsessed with keeping children with their birth mothers. The longer these youngsters remain in state institutions, in the hope that one

day their birth mothers will reclaim them, the more difficult it eventually becomes to place them. Surely with the care system being in the mess it has been, this is simply not good enough for our most vulnerable children. And we know, too, that there are many good parents who cannot get any babies to adopt.

So let us at least consider what Straw has suggested. But no – even a debate on this subject is such heresy that our experts would torch our words before we can speak.

Perhaps I should be a little kinder to these people. They can't help being insanely protective of their ideologies and procedures, because such a wash of emotion overcomes thought whenever the subject is raised. Adoption highlights the perennial conflicts between nature and nurture, the powerful and the powerless, rights and responsibilities. It generates poignant stories of secrets and lies. It flashes up the dynamics of sex, race and class. It is the stuff of fairy tales and fables and the terrors of childhood.

For years, a wicked older cousin used to make me cry by telling me that I was found on the roadside, ant-bitten, in a torn basket, on the road to Entebbe, and that my parents took pity and adopted me. It was easy to believe him because, when I was born, all the rooms in my father's heart were already taken up or shut down. So this was why Papa never hugged me, I thought.

I look around the scattered field that contains our two families, one English and one Ugandan Asian, and there are least two known stories of unwanted pregnancy and adoption. A child was forcibly taken away from a wild teenage mother in the Fifties, never to be heard of again. Her one photograph has disappeared. Forty-five years have passed but the pain of not knowing remains, although the matter is never discussed. In contrast, another teenager refused to have her child taken into adoption and stuck with it. The child is bright and contented, but the tough times her mother went through have taken a terrible toll.

The past was indeed a bad land for teenagers who found themselves pregnant; shame combined with a complete lack of others' compassion to make life unspeakably punishing. Giving up babies in that atmo-sphere was, I imagine, a relief; and at least the conspiracy of silence stopped the noises of accusations and demanding, oppressive questions. Being forced back into their own heads, however, drove a third of them half mad with guilt and hopelessness. But this is not the past.

What happened in the Fifties and Sixties – when each year more than 20,000 babies were taken away by mothers, nuns or matrons – is not

---

The whole area of adoption needs to be transformed so that we can discuss the issues in an informed way

---

what happens today. Nor could it because that pervasive sense of shame has dissolved for ever. We also have an openness, and access to post-adoption information. To say then that what Straw was suggesting is a return to the Fifties is completely wrong-headed.

Felicity Collier, for example, director of the British Agencies for Adoption and Fostering, evokes the ghosts of times long past whenever a radical shift in thinking on adoption is suggested. Too many others involved in the business do this too. The maddest among them even believe in a class plot to take away the children of the poor, and Blair making speeches about expanding the middle class has probably reinforced this paranoia.

Dare to suggest, as I have done, that same-race adoptions, although highly desirable, cannot be the only driving principle for the placement of children, and you have to go into hiding. Getting such a child in care brought up by good black and Asian parents would be the best thing of all. But we should not pretend that

ethnicity bestows parentcraft. There are appalling black and Asian parents to whom I would not give a dead cat to mind, and white parents who not only give their non-white adoptive children a nurturing home, but work very hard to provide them with an appropriate cultural and racial identity.

Again, in the past there were massive failures where black children were placed in inappropriate white homes in all-white areas. And it is because black social workers and the wife of Paul Boateng fought for a change, that we learnt about this. The sad thing is that blindness was substituted by deafness as experts and practitioners set about replacing an unworkable old orthodoxy (All you need is love) with a new one (What's love got to do with it? All you need is black skin). Yet when Boateng brought this up last year, just as now, the troops of social workers, BAAF et al came out holding up their banners of no change.

Returning to teenage mothers, it is right that adoption should be offered as a positive choice. The number of these pregnancies is higher than in any other EU country. Most of the girls are under-educated and have few prospects. As the Louise Woodward case shows, looking after a small child when you are very young yourself can be deadly.

Economic deprivation makes this all the harder. Many teenagers regret their pregnancies because they know how hard is the endless journey ahead. Suggesting that they might get better guidance on adoption is not to stigmatise them but to offer them real options, and to take away the negative image of adoption. From being the good guys who were offering homes to children in need, adoptive parents have been made to feel that they are taking children away from their birthright.

The whole area of adoption needs to be transformed so that we can discuss the issues in an informed way. If we can achieve that, then perhaps we can then start to treat radical new ideas as opportunities and not threats to be fought off whatever the cost.

I hope Sally doesn't hate me

Lisa was 19 when she gave up her baby for adoption. She and her mother tell Elizabeth Grice about their decision

There is no such thing as a simple adoption. However careful the preparations, however conscientious the post-adoption procedures, human emotions have a way of throwing up complexities that defy all precedent and experience.

Lisa Hornchurch was a baffling case from the beginning. A quiet, introspective girl of 18, she somehow managed to conceal her pregnancy from her parents and her boyfriend for eight months. Until very late in the day, she seems hardly to have acknowledged it herself.

In the short time between admitting the pregnancy and the onset of labour, she decided to have the child adopted, believing it was 'for the best'. But once the baby was in her arms, her emotions swung violently between wanting to keep her child and needing to let her go. Now 18 months old, Sally is happily settled with her adoptive parents, but Lisa is still in turmoil.

Once the baby had been given up, she could not bear to 'carry on as before' with the father of her child – and in any case, she knew the relationship would not last. Being accepted for a university place was one of the reasons why she decided not to keep the child – but in the ensuing emotional upheaval, she lost the ability to concentrate and has now abandoned the course.

Lisa's secrecy about the pregnancy effectively barred her from any form of counselling or help. Anxious that others should not become so isolated, she has joined TALKadoption, a new national helpline for under-25s who are linked in any way with adoption. At the start of Adoption Week, Lisa and her mother, Christine, explain how they are living with the hardest decision they have ever had to make.

Lisa's story

My boyfriend and I met in 1995 when we were 17. He lived in another part of the country and we only saw each other every couple of weeks. We were using contraception but we were unlucky. I never told him about the baby.

Towards the end, he knew there was something wrong, but I couldn't explain over the phone. He didn't know about the pregnancy until three days before Sally was born, when he got my letter. He didn't write back and he didn't tell his mum and dad.

I don't know how I managed to keep the secret because I didn't hide away. I just carried on with my life, blocking it out, hoping things would be all right. I wore the same baggy clothes I always wore and the same jeans I wear now. I even went swimming. If I had stopped doing the things I always did, I would have drawn attention to myself. But as the months went by, I seemed to be looking at myself the whole time, positioning myself so that no one would notice me. All the time, you're looking at people's faces… it was a horrible way to live.

My mum asked me quite a few times whether I was pregnant but I always denied it. The month before Sally was born, she asked me one last time and I told the truth. She was worried and sympathetic – but quite calm, really. She never blamed me.

I just could not have faced having an abortion. That's probably why I kept the baby a secret. Somebody would have tried to persuade me to have it aborted.

A few hours after Sally was born, I came home, leaving her in hospital. It was not a nice day. The nurses had taken some photographs of me with her and when my mum and I showed them to my younger brother, he accused us of lying and messing about: it was someone else's baby. He didn't believe us until the midwife came.

I didn't make any sensible decisions about what to do until she was born, and right up to the adoption hearing, three months later, my mind changed so many times. In the end, I decided to have her adopted because I was too young – only just 19 – and I was living at home.

It seemed to me that adoption

would give her a better chance in life. Maybe I was afraid of being tied down. There are five of us in this small house already, so there was not enough room for another one. I had also been offered a place at university.

We took a lot of photographs of Sally because I want her to know that she had a life before being fostered and then adopted. Now, I write to her all the time. I tell her everything. The letters will be there for her in the future. They are not sealed, so nothing is hidden from her adoptive parents.

I keep a book for her, listing everything we have given her – blankets, toys, teddies, clothes. I've had a letter from her adoptive parents – they do realise I am a mum as well – so I know what her words were at the time they wrote to me. She was holding on to furniture, nearly walking… but I don't know what she's saying now, or when she started crawling or what teddies she picks up.

My boyfriend came to see Sally in the foster home last year but I have not seen him since. I knew that our relationship could not carry on if she was to be adopted. It either had to be over or we all had to be together. But I knew he wasn't the person I wanted to be with for the rest of my life.

I would never want to keep what has happened a secret from another boyfriend. Sally's photographs are all over my bedroom and when I am upset, he'd have to know why.

Last summer, university was my goal, but it's as if now that she's out of my life I don't have to do the things I said I would do. I gave up my university course at the end of the first year because I couldn't concentrate. I've just lost it for studying.

Still, I don't want to put the clock back. I wouldn't wish not to have had her because she's… so nice. I think about her from the moment I wake up to the moment I go to bed. I just want her to understand what my life was like at the time and I hope she doesn't hate me for what I have done. It was the right thing to do then.

Christine's story

At first, I joked that Lisa was putting on weight. She always wore a fleece and big, baggy sweatshirts, so it was not difficult to disguise what was happening. When I asked her outright if she was pregnant, she denied it, saying I was neurotic. I felt neurotic.

One day, I arranged to meet her in town. It was a hot day and she got off the bus wearing a T-shirt, I knew. We went for a coffee and I said: 'I just want an answer: yes or no.' At home, she would have walked out and gone to her room but we were in a café and she couldn't blow up. She just said: 'Yes'.

I don't know what I felt; it was like a dream. I felt sick, and disappointed that she hadn't told me. We never got to the bottom of why she didn't confide in us. We never asked her. There seems no point now.

We went straight down to see my husband at work. He erupted to begin with and I was very upset. But he soon calmed down and since then he has just wanted to protect Lisa. He said she didn't deserve it – and she didn't – because she is not an irresponsible girl.

I was worried about her health and the health of the baby, so we went to our doctor immediately. We did not know it at the time, but there were only two weeks to go before the birth.

Sally was born after three and a half hours' labour. The cord was round her neck and I imagined what could have happened if Lisa had tried to deliver the baby herself in secret. She was marvellous, she had no drugs and was very controlled.

It was a totally confusing time. Lisa was almost certain she wanted to have the baby adopted, but she just wanted to scoop the baby up and bring her home. We held her and bottle-fed her and visited her regularly. When Sally was three months old, her foster parents asked if we would like to bring her home for the day. We took a video of her and lots of photos. Soon after, Lisa made up her mind that adoption was

---

I just want her to understand what my life was like at the time and I hope she doesn't hate me for what I have done

---

the right thing. We presented her with all the possible choices. She didn't feel she could give the baby all she wanted to give.

My husband and I had to face the fact that we didn't want to be parents again – and she didn't want to place that burden on us. We have two teenage sons as well. Looking at Sally, we just wanted to keep her but we had to think of five years' time, 10 years' time.

Lisa was adamant that she did not want to live with her boyfriend. They registered the birth together and he and his family send clothes and things.

Sometimes, I feel as if I'm walking a tightrope. I have to support Lisa because she's been through a massive emotional crisis – but at the same time, I have my own feelings for Sally to deal with and so does my husband.

I also have to make sure the boys are having a normal existence. At times, I have to be a very good actress. One of the things that keeps me going is the thought that her adoptive parents desperately wanted a baby and could not have had one but for Lisa. One day, I hope we will all meet up.

There are still moments of utter despair, thinking about Sally and wanting her here. But we know she has got a wonderful new family and that it was all 'for the best'. Sally gave us a lot of joy in that short time. It hasn't been all doom and gloom.

There's never a day goes by when I don't think of her. But I've got to keep in my mind that the decision we made was right for that time. We've lived and talked through everything we've done. We don't want her to grow up hating us. We want her to know she had a loving past from the moment she was born.

All names have been changed.

• TALKadoption is the first national helpline for young people who are adopted or linked with adoption. Its trained volunteers can be contacted on Tuesdays, Wednesdays and Thursdays from 3 to 9pm. Calls are free and taken in confidence on 0800 783 1234.

TALKadoption

A helpline for young people

What is TALKadoption?

TALKadoption is the national telephone helpline for young people, up to 25 years old, who have a link with adoption. It is the only national service about adoption for young people.

Callers include:

- adopted people
- birth parents whose children have been or may be adopted
- brothers and sisters from the birth family
- brothers and sisters from the adoptive family
- friends of people involved in adoption

A friendly ear to young people . . .

Calls are answered by a team of trained voluntary staff, recruited for their ability to listen and offer support to young people on the telephone. The emphasis of TALKadoption is to give relevant information and offer a friendly ear to young people, who often feel they have no one they can talk to about adoption, just at the time when they are beginning to explore the meaning of life.

Reaching young people . . .

TALKadoption is a project of the Post Adoption Forum, a consortium of charities who work with people, after adoption has taken place. The Forum recognised from their experiences that young people were not contacting the existing services. They decided to create a national telephone helpline as this is a good medium for reaching young people. By also offering a freephone service the helpline gives wide accessibility to a group of people who often have very limited income.

Funding

The initial funding for TALKadoption is via a grant from the National Lottery Charities Board. The project is seeking ongoing funding.

Paid staff

A small team of paid staff carry out all organisational duties, including planning, training, publicity and policy development and are responsible for the running of the helpline and the team of voluntary staff.

Professional steering group

TALKadoption is based in Manchester at the home of After Adoption, who are leading the project on behalf of the Post Adoption Forum. TALKadoption is overseen by a Steering Group consisting of Post Adoption Forum members, user representatives and professionals from a range of related fields. User input is also gained via an advisory Group and through the helpline's newsletter *TALKnews*, which is offered to callers who wish to go on the mailing list, and is also distributed to a variety of agencies nation-wide.

Voluntary staff

Voluntary staff come from a wide variety of backgrounds. The helpline tries to recruit a team which balances many life experiences including age, gender, culture, and experience of adoption (about two-thirds of the team have personal experience of adoption).

Helpline staff follow policies and guidelines covering such topics as confidentiality (and how to break it if there are serious concerns that the caller is at risk), and how to deal with calls that staff may find difficult or upsetting. All calls are anonymously recorded. The helpline is a member of the Telephone Helplines Association, which promotes good practice amongst helpline providers.

A unique position . . .

TALKadoption is in a unique position to contribute to the development of adoption practice and knowledge by the experience and information gained from directly working with young people.

Training

TALKadoption staff undergo a specialist training programme aimed at developing voluntary helpers' listening skills and their ability to be empathic with young callers.

Training in adoption issues covers a wide variety of topics including:

- adoption law and procedures throughout the UK
- the lifelong impact of adoption
- the emotional impact of adoption
- identity formation
- current practice issues
- specific issues facing young people

All helpline staff take part in individual and group supervision sessions and ongoing training to develop skills and knowledge.

TALKadoption is the national helpline for young people, up to 25 years old, who have a link with adoption, whether they are adopted, have given a child for adoption, or are relatives or friends of adopted people.

- TALKadoption is a free, confidential service: 0808 808 1234. Tuesday to Friday 3pm to 9pm.

© *TALKadoption*

The mother of all meetings

Many adopted children trace their natural parents – but Sam Edwards went one step further and arranged the riskiest of get-togethers. Judith Woods hears how two mothers became good friends

'Come into the living room and meet my mums,' says Sam Edwards, a petite redhead in jeans and T-shirt. She strides across the hallway and opens the door with a flourish.

The two women stand politely as I am introduced. Kitty, in hippy sandals and baggy russet cardigan, bears a marked resemblance to Sam – the same shade of pale red hair, a similar cast to the nose and smile. It is less easy to make an instant connection between Sam and Pamela, whose finely spun white hair and green trouser suit suggest a different generation and way of life.

'I refer to them as my Hove mum and my Ick mum, because Kitty lives in Hove and Pamela lives in Ickenham,' explains Sam cheerily, as the two women sit down; red Hove mum settling into the sofa and white Ick mum selecting the straight-backed chair. Sam, who looks younger than her 28 years, sprawls on a harlequin-patterned floor cushion.

'I don't see this as an either/or situation, about where my loyalties lie,' she says. 'I have two mums and it's as simple – or as complicated – as that.'

For Sam, basking in maternal attention, this may be a straightforward state of affairs, but the friendship that has developed between Pamela and Kitty is, by any standards, an extraordinary one. Pamela is Sam's adoptive mother and has cared for her since the age of three and a half months. Kitty is Sam's natural mother and re-entered her life only 18 months ago.

Each year, hundreds of people in Britain are reunited with their natural relatives by a process of tentative reconciliation that can have painful repercussions. A sense of rivalry – whether openly acknowledged or not – between adoptive and birth mothers is a natural corollary of the emotional upheaval.

But while a satisfactory *modus vivendi* is often reached, even the adoption authorities concede that the instant rapport between Pamela and Kitty is exceptional.

Kitty was a 15-year-old schoolgirl, back in 1969, when she discovered she was pregnant by her 19-year-old boyfriend. Too terrified to tell her parents, she concealed her condition for as long as she could, playing hockey and other sports late into the sixth month of her pregnancy.

'When my parents found out, they were horrified at the shame I had brought on the family,' she says. 'My father pushed me away from him. My mother was just terribly anxious to get rid of me before anyone found out. I was quickly packed off to my grandmother in Islington, and it was decided the baby would be adopted. I was given no choice.'

When labour began, Kitty was expected to take herself to the hospital. She boarded a bus, and had to stand for the entire journey, enduring disapproving glances. The birth itself was long and difficult, and distressing for a naïve teenager who had been given no idea what to expect.

She cared for her daughter for 10 days before she was taken away and placed with foster parents. On their final morning together, Kitty had just finished dressing Sam in the ward when a social worker arrived. There was no time for a tender goodbye.

'The woman seemed to be very impatient, so I just handed Sam over to her. I followed them both to the lift and, as the door closed, I realised I would never see my baby again. I felt devastated, but I couldn't cry. I hung about the ward for a while, then I just caught the bus home.'

She had no further contact with the child's father; the relationship had broken up while she was in the early months of pregnancy and, thereafter, she was forbidden from seeing him. The baby was never again discussed at home.

At 30, Kitty married and had a second daughter, Georgia. The marriage lasted just four and a half years and, in 1993, Kitty married again. She told both her husbands about Sam, but despite their sympathy, she had constant feelings of 'isolation'.

'I felt heartbroken,' she says. 'My husbands were supportive, but there was always an underlying sense of sadness and tremendous loss. It was terrible when my daughter Georgia was born – I became so clingy towards

her. All the time, I wondered what Sam was doing, and what she looked like – but I had no information of any sort.'

The baby was fostered for more than three months before she was finally handed over for adoption by Pamela and her husband Dennis, an advertising copywriter. The couple, both in their early thirties, had applied to adopt after unsuccessfully trying for a family of their own.

'We always told Sam she was adopted,' says Pamela. 'We used to make up bed-time stories about rabbits who had adopted little bunnies, and I used to say that she was specially chosen from lots and lots of other babies.'

Sam interjects excitedly: 'I only found out that wasn't true about a year ago, when someone else who'd been adopted said: "Did they feed you the old line about being specially chosen?" I couldn't believe you'd lied all those years!'

Sam and Kitty erupt into giggles, egging each other on like schoolgirls. Pamela patiently waits for them to settle down before continuing.

'It was the only lie we *ever* told,' she says gravely. 'We were told it was for the best. The information we had about Sam's mother was that she was the middle of five children, and was fair-ish and pretty-ish with blue eyes. The file also said Kitty liked reading romantic novels.'

'I was completely affronted when Pamela told me about that file,' says Kitty. 'It makes me sound so flaky; it was lies!' She is about to hold forth further, but suddenly seems to become aware that she might be upstaging Pamela.

'I very much wanted to know how Kitty was doing,' continues Pamela. 'I was aware of how young she was, and that her parents had turned her out. I wrote to the Children's Society asking for news of her, but it wasn't their policy to give any information.'

Sam's childhood was happy and uneventful. An academically minded schoolgirl, she had a love of music and a flair for drawing. She was to discover that she shared both traits with her natural mother.

It was not until Sam was in her mid-twenties and working as a computer operator in London that she decided she had the time and 'space' in her life to track down Kitty. National figures show this is typical; the majority of adopted children are between 25 and 35 when they begin to trace their biological parents.

'Those bunny stories must have paid off because, as a child, I never felt uncomfortable about being adopted,' says Sam. 'I didn't spend hours dreaming of my "real" mother, but I was curious.'

When Sam contacted the Children's Society, she learnt that there was a letter in her file from Kitty, which had lain there for six years. It gave an address, in the event that her daughter wished to contact her.

Sam's adoptive mother had told her that she would help her find her natural mother. But, in the event, Sam decided she wanted to conduct her search alone. Pamela claims she experienced no feelings of rejection or jealousy.

'Sam has always been a very sensible person, and my love for her is such that she has always had my support,' she says firmly. 'I've always placed Sam and her interests first. I remember I was very impressed that Clare Short and her son had found one another and how fulfilled they seemed.'

At this point, Kitty starts to giggle: 'Ooh, it's become very fashionable, finding your long lost relatives,' she says, pulling a face at Sam. 'We're *so* fashionable!'

Sam and Kitty's slightly frantic infatuation is palpable. Sam gazes up at her as Kitty speaks, they prompt each other, embellish each other's anecdotes and share the same loud, resonant laugh. It is a sound that fills the small room – an expression of shared amusement that excludes others, however unintentionally.

Pamela follows their animated exchanges from the periphery, an unassailably serene expression on her face. Every so often, Sam casts a swift, concerned glance up at her, attempting to gauge her responses to the banter, reassuring her she is not forgotten.

Yet it is clear that Pamela is not dissembling when she denies feelings of rivalry. When Sam considered writing to Kitty, she was encouraged by her adoptive mother.

'The first letter I sent was quite short,' says Sam. 'I just wrote a bit about what I was doing now, rather than attempting to squeeze 26 years of my life on to a few pages.'

The letter was posted late in 1996. Kitty describes her reaction as 'Elation followed by tears and more tears. I thought: "Oh God, she may hate me – what if I find her and then lose her again?"'

A few more letters were exchanged before Kitty telephoned Sam, and mother and daughter spoke for the first time. Neither can recall exactly what they talked about, other than 'mundane, everyday things'.

'I remember laughing so much,' says Sam. 'We talked for about an hour and a half, and my hand was sore because I'd been clutching the receiver so tightly.'

Kitty wobbles her arms about to illustrate the fact that she felt 'like jelly'. Yet for all the badinage, the rawness of her emotion is clear. Her eyes fill with tears intermittently and, at one point, she reaches out and touches Pamela gently on the arm, who smiles comfortingly.

The first meeting between Sam and Kitty came just before Christmas 1996. Sam drove to Kitty's home in Hove.

'I was hiding in the kitchen before Sam arrived,' says Kitty. 'I'd been cooking a lunch of home-made soup and lemon meringue pie, and I was horribly nervous. When she appeared at the front door, we both just screamed and hugged and cried and *flapped*.'

'There was a *lot* of flapping,' Sam confirms, with an indulgent grin.

Kitty admits she probably overwhelmed Sam: 'I made her eat lunch and fussed over her and showed her far too many photos of my massive family. I couldn't get over how *little* Sam was.'

Mother and daughter stayed in contact, visiting and telephoning each other, and Sam was introduced to her half-sister Georgia, who had previously not known of her existence.

Seven months later, on her 28th birthday, Sam arranged what she refers to as 'The Meeting of the Mums,' in her Wimbledon flat. Sam was confident the two women would get on well. Pamela was sanguine. Kitty was angst-ridden.

'I was an absolute wreck; I so much wanted Pamela to like me that I brought her a huge bunch of flowers,' recalls Kitty.

'If it went badly, I knew it would create so many tensions.'

Tears are welling up in Kitty's eyes again: 'It's not a personal thing, but knowing that someone else has known Sam and loved her, and that I can never have that, is very difficult. But I'm happy because Pamela has loved Sam so much.'

Since that first meeting, Pamela and Kitty have kept in touch with occasional telephone calls, letters and visits. When Pamela's own mother died, Kitty and her husband volunteered to help clear out the house.

Pamela says Kitty turned out to be more or less as she had imagined her. 'I suppose, in my mind's eye, I still see Kitty as a schoolgirl who had a baby, and my feelings towards her are maternal rather than competitive.'

'I do think of her as Sam's mother, but sometimes she seems more like her older sister.'

Kitty, on the other hand, regards Pamela as a mother-in-law figure. Yet with acquaintances, she will refer to her, confusingly, as 'my eldest daughter's mother'.

'As far as I'm concerned, Pamela *is* Sam's mum – she brought her up. And if you bring up a child, you have a special relationship with it.

'To be honest, I think I would have struggled with this whole thing had I been in Pamela's position. If it hadn't been for her acceptance of me, things would have turned out very differently.'

There is a quiver in Kitty's voice as she speaks. Pamela turns to her with a look of affection and responds softly: 'Far from losing a daughter, I feel like I've gained a family, with Kitty and Sandy and Georgia.'

• *Preparing for Reunion: Experiences from the Adoption Circle* (published by the Children's Society) discusses the different scenarios that can result when adopted people search for their birth relatives. It is available for £7.95 post free (UK) from Telegraph Books Direct, 24 Seward Street, London EC1V 3GB or call 0541 557222.

The campaign for relatives' rights

Adoption charities have just launched a campaign for a change in the law to give natural mothers the right to information about children they give up for adoption. An estimated 750,000 women have had children adopted since the procedure was produced in 1926.

At present, blood relatives have no legal right to see records, nor even to learn whether the child is alive. Some local authorities and charities, such as the Children's Society, give natural mothers access to information, providing the information cannot be used to identify or trace the adopted person. Agencies may also have a policy of acting as intermediaries by passing on messages from blood relatives to adults who have been adopted.

The Children's Society, the Catholic Children's Society (Westminster) and the West Midlands Post Adoption Service have called on Lord Irvine, the Lord Chancellor, to put forward legislation to give blood relatives the right to see adoption records. The charities also want all blood relatives to have the right to contact adopted adults through an intermediary service.

If you are a blood relative and want to find out more about an adopted person there are a number of steps you can take.

- You should get in touch with the agency that placed the child for adoption in order to find out whether it provides an intermediary service for blood relatives.
- If your child was placed for adoption by the Children's Society, contact Julia Feast at the Post Adoption and Care Project, 91-93 Queen's Road, Peckham, London SE15 2EZ.
- You can place your name on the Adoption Contact Register at the Office for National Statistics: tel. 0151 471 4586.
- Contact the Natural Parents' Network at 3 Ashdown Drive, Mosley Common, near Tyldesley, Manchester M28 1BR.
- Norcap, the National Organisation for the Counselling of Adoptees and Parents, will help trace adopted adults and act as an intermediary: 112 Church Road, Wheatley, Oxfordshire OX33 1LU.

Babies' four-year wait for adoption

By Glenda Cooper

More than half of children who are adopted were given up as babies but it takes an average four years before a new family is found according to research published today.

Urgent examination of why such delays take place is needed, said the British Agencies for Adoption and Fostering which added the figures were 'shocking', leaving too many children in a 'sad and vulnerable position'.

The BAAF published *Children Adopted From Care*, the first analysis of information on children adopted out of public care in England during 1995/6, to coincide with the start of National Adoption Week. It found that more than half of those adopted came into care before the age of one and half of these were in the first month of their life. Only one in ten of the children adopted had entered care aged five or over.

It took on average four years before the children were adopted. Children waited nearly two years before they were placed with the families which would later adopt them and a further two years before the adoption order was made. One in six children freed for adoption had still not been placed with adoptive families two years later.

A case of mixed blessings

Families will face more rigorous checks if they want to adopt overseas, reports Sarah Wellard

Twelve-year-old Amy Wordley has no problem about being a black child from Peru adopted by a white family. She thinks the problem lies with other people, like those who stare at her when she's out with her family. 'Why should I feel uneasy?' she asks. 'I'm just like any of them, just a different colour'.

Yet despite the success stories, where children who would otherwise have languished in third world or eastern European orphanages adjust well to becoming British citizens with white relatives, intercountry adoption is still seen as a somewhat shady business. The practice is poorly regulated and perceived as being more about finding babies for childless couples than meeting the needs of children. In the worst instances there are questions about the consent of birth relatives, or parents being paid to give up their children. And intercountry adoption is often frowned upon by social workers because it usually means black and ethnic minority children being placed with white families.

A private member's bill sponsored by the Labour MP Mark Oaten aims to address some of these concerns. The bill, which received its second reading on Friday, seeks to ratify the Hague Convention on Protection of Children and Co-operation in Respect of Intercountry Adoption, making the whole process more child-focused.

If it becomes law it will be a criminal offence to bring a child into this country for adoption without following the correct legal procedures. And prospective adopters will be subject to the same tests and assessments as they would be if adopting a British child.

Felicity Collier, director of British Agencies for Adoption and Fostering, is hopeful that the bill will help root out illegal practices. She says: 'We shouldn't have a two-tier system just because some children come from poor and disadvantaged countries.'

Yet it won't address the fundamental contradiction between intercountry adoption and domestic adoption, where the philosophy is about finding parents for children. Ratna Dutt, director of the Race Equality Unit, points out: 'In an ideal world parents would be matched to children needing families, not the other way round.' But the cost of adopting from abroad – often as much as £10,000 by the time you allow for travel expenses, legal costs and adoption agency fees – means that most adopters are middle class and white.

But there are instances – perhaps 40 or 50 a year – where people from ethnic minorities adopt an unrelated child from their country of origin. Take for example Mei-Mei Towlsom, who is seeking to adopt a child from China or Hong Kong. An inter-country adoptee herself, she says she has no regrets about being brought up in the UK by a white family, and wants to give another child the opportunities she's had. She says: 'Of course I've encountered racism, especially as a child at school. If you're different people will pick on you. But we've always been a close and very secure family, and I was brought up to be proud of what I am.'

Daruni Jones, a 20-year-old adoptee from Thailand, agrees that having an adoptive family who are positive about your ethnic identity and whom you can talk to about the racism you experience is a key factor in how well intercountry adoptees come to accept their situation.

Daruni's German Jewish mother, who adopted her from a Bangkok orphanage at the age of 16 months, knows herself what it is like to be the victim of racist abuse.

In July, the day after she finishes her finals, Daruni, together with her mother, her grandmother and her sister – who is also a Thai adoptee but not a blood relative – are all flying to Thailand. It's Daruni's second visit, and this time she will be the guest of the Thai adoption agency, along with a group of other intercountry adoptees.

Daruni says the trip means a great deal to her, even though she knows that there is no chance of tracing her birth mother. 'It's a part of me I can't ignore,' she says.

As a teenager she found it hard to come to terms with the fact that she'd been abandoned. 'I used to get really upset at birthdays,' she recalls. 'I'd look at the stars and wonder if my mother was there.'

• First published in *The Guardian*, April, 1999.   © Sarah Wellard

A question of trust

Henrietta Bond finds support for adoptive parents of 'difficult' babies

James was a premature baby who spent the first four months of his life in hospital. When his adoptive mother, Moira, took him home she was told to 'treat him as normal'.

'I've had children of my own and many foster children, but nothing in my experience had prepared me for such a difficult baby,' Moira says. 'He had tantrums where I could hardly hold him. He wasn't interested in anything around him and went into a world of his own.'

James is now nine years old and needs constant reassurance of his adopted parents' affection. Moira feels that, by acting on her instincts, she has 'forged an attachment, although he fought me all the way'. She spent a lot of time rocking and stroking him, allowed him to have baby things beyond the normal age, and established reassuring routines. But it was not until Moira came into contact with the Parent to Parent Information on Adoption Services (PPIAS) attachment support network that she began to understand the root of James's difficulties.

She says: 'People don't believe that new-born babies can suffer harm by being separated from their birth mothers, but I've met adoptive parents of so-called "perfect" babies who've had major problems. I'm lucky that, although James has his problems, we have established a relationship and people say he loves me to bits. That's so much better than the "china doll" – the completely withdrawn, unattached child many adopters have to live with.'

The PPIAS network supports more than 300 families whose children have attachment difficulties of some kind, but describes this as the tip of the iceberg. Attachment difficulties occur for many reasons. These include: trauma in the womb; the trauma of separation; physical and psychological pain of early medical intervention; or the effects of abuse or neglect. The network is keen to help parents to address potential attachment difficulties before they occur or develop further.

Caroline Archer is the co-ordinator of the attachment support network and author of *Parenting the Child Who Hurts*. As an adoptive parent, she has carried out a great deal of research into attachment difficulties and trauma, has discovered many techniques which worked with her own children, and has collated a great deal of information from other adoptive parents. Many of these techniques focus on stimulating the child's awareness of his senses and allowing the child times when he can regress to babyhood.

Attachment difficulties occur for many reasons. These include: trauma in the womb; the trauma of separation; or the effects of abuse or neglect

---

Archer explains that a baby who learns that his mother – with whom he is so closely connected from the womb – is there to comfort him when he cries can begin to trust another human being to meet his needs. Without this reassurance, a child may begin to overreact to every minor emotional trigger and can lose the ability to discriminate between feelings, so even benign experiences appear threatening.

'As adoptive parents you want to get "right back" before the time of trauma and help new patterns of arousal and calming to be laid down to give the child a better foundation,' Archer explains. 'One of the important things is communicating with your child through touch, movement, eye contact, smell and tone of voice – all the ways babies and their mothers communicate together. This has potential for all parents; if there is already an attachment it will enhance the child's overall development and self-esteem.'

Louise is an adoptive parent who has used many of the techniques from Archer's book to help overcome her son's initial resistance to eye contact and being cuddled. Louise would cradle 16-month-old Samuel in her arms, following his roaming eyes around the room until she could eventually get him to look at her. She played many games of 'peek-a-boo' and would stroke him lightly on his cheek or blow on his face gently, to gain his attention. Samuel would giggle and blow back. Within six months he had established eye contact.

Samuel also wanted to be in control at all times and Louise needed to show him how to depend on her for comfort. She became his 'prime carer', always the one to bath and put him to bed. She ensured that she was always there to pick him up if he fell over, and soon he started coming to her for comfort.

'A friend who saw him at 16 months, then more recently, said he seemed so much happier and contented,' Louise says. 'She noticed how he now looks back at me when he does things. Unattached children often get praised for independence, but they don't care if they run off and get lost. An attached child who gets lost bawls his eyes out and wants to be cuddled.'

The names of adopters and children in this article have been changed.

Parenting the Child Who Hurts, by Caroline Archer, is available from PPIAS (telephone: 01327-260295).

• First published in *The Guardian*, April, 1998.   © *Henrietta Bond*

ADDITIONAL RESOURCES

You might like to contact the following organisations for further information. Due to the increasing cost of postage, many organisations cannot respond to enquiries unless they receive a stamped, addressed envelope.

Adoption and Fostering Information Line (AFIL)
193 Market Street
Hyde
Cheshire, SK14 1HF
Tel: 0800 783 4086
Web sites: www.adoption.org.uk
www.fostering.org.uk
The Adoption Information Line and its sister service The Fostering Information Line assist local authority social services departments and adoption agencies to recruit carers for the children they have identified as being in need of foster care or adoption placements. Produces a student information pack, covering information from a range of organisations in this field, costing £5.95.

Adoption UK
Lower Boddington
Daventry
Northamptonshire, NN11 6YB
Tel: 01327 260295
Fax: 01327 263565
Works to provide support, through a nation-wide network of adoptive families, for established adoptive parents and to help potential adopters. Produces useful literature on adoption issues.

Barnardo's
Tanners Lane
Barkingside
Ilford
Essex, IG6 1QG
Tel: 0181 550 8822
Fax: 0181 551 6870
Web site: www.barnardos.org.uk
Works to help each person to achieve his or her potential. This can mean helping a young person with a learning disability to live and work in the community, or working with families under stress to help them to enjoy a stable and caring family home.

British Agencies for Adoption and Fostering (BAAF)
Skyline House
200 Union Street
London, SE1 0LX
Tel: 0171 593 2000
Fax: 0171 593 2001
E-mail: mail@baaf.org.uk
Web site: www.baaf.org.uk
Promotes the interests of children separated from their families by taking a lead in the field of adoption and fostering. Produces new research, practice guidance and information leaflets.

NCH Action for Children
85 Highbury Park
London, N5 1UD
Tel: 0171 226 2033
Fax: 0171 226 2537
Web site: www.nchafc.org.uk
NCH Action For Children improves the lives of Britains most vulnerable children and young people by providing a diverse and innovative range of services for them and their families and campaigning on their behalf.

Overseas Adoption Helpline
PO Box 13899
London, N6 4WB
Tel: 0990 168742
Fax: 0181 348 1522
Overseas Adoption Helpline is a confidential information and advice service on intercountry adoption. The Helpline is a registered charity and is a member of the Telephone Helplines Association, the International Forum for Child Welfare and European Forum for Child Welfare.

Parents for Children
41 Southgate Road
London, N1 3JP
Tel: 0171 359 7530
Fax: 0171 226 7840
Places children of exceptional need in permanent foster and adoptive families.

Post-Adoption Centre
5 Torriano Mews
Torriano Avenue
London, NW5 2RZ
Tel: 0171 284 0555
Fax: 0171 482 2367
Offers a post-adoption support and counselling service for adoptive people and birth parents whose child was adopted, and works for an improved public understanding of adoption.

TALKadoption
12 Chapel Street
Manchester, M3 7NN
Tel: 0161 819 2345
Fax: 0161 832 2242
E-mail: admin@talkadoption.org.uk
Web site: www.talkadoption.org.uk
TALKadoption is the national helpline for young people, up to 25 years old, who have a link with adoption, whether they are adopted, have given a child for adoption, or are relatives or friends of adopted people. TALKadoption is a free, confidential service on 0808 808 1234, Tuesday to Friday 3pm to 9pm.

INDEX

The Internet has been likened to shopping in a supermarket without aisles. The press of a button on a Web browser can bring up thousands of sites but working your way through them to find what you want can involve long and frustrating on-line searches.

And unfortunately many sites contain inaccurate, misleading or heavily biased information. Our researchers have therefore undertaken an extensive analysis to bring you a selection of quality Web site addresses.

* * * * *

Adoption and Fostering Information Line (AFIL)
www.adoption.org.uk
The most popular internet site on adoption within the UK. In their very first year of being on-line they have had over 22,000 visitors. The popularity of these pages confirms the need for clear and friendly advice on this subject, a need AFIL is trying to meet. The site is organised into various categories including: 1. Information pages – These contain a wealth of information upon a wide variety of topics concerning adoption, just keep selecting the next page from the left. For a specific subject, visit their index from the left. 2. Children's features – Learn about individual children for whom placements are currently being sought and get a rough idea of what it might be like if they were to become a member of your family. 3. News and views – The latest news about adoption issues and also some contributions from others. Learn how being adopted has affected someone, the good and the not so good.

Adoption and Fostering Information Line (AFIL)
www.fostering.org.uk
This site is organised into various categories which can be selected from the left navigation bar. The categories include: 1. Information pages – The pages in this section are of two types: first information pages which are intended to provide a good general knowledge about fostering and foster care; and advanced topic pages which are more detailed and most likely to be of interest to social workers, experienced foster carers and newcomers who are wanting

information on one of the specific topics covered. The advanced topic category can be entered through their index. 2. Children's features – Learn about individual children for whom placements are currently being sought and learn what it might be like to have them as part of your household. 3. News and views – The latest news about foster care and contributions from existing foster carers as well as from those who are or have been in foster care.

Adoption InterLink UK
www.argonet.co.uk/users/adopt
Adoption InterLink UK is for anyone who has an interest in and who is looking for information and contacts about the multi-faceted experiences and needs that are part of the adoption process. Just click on Straight to Contents for a wide range of information and contacts.

British Agencies for Adoption and Fostering (BAAF)
www.baaf.org.uk
BAAF helps find permanent new families for children who, for a variety of reasons, cannot live with their birth families. Their family finding services link children needing permanent placements with prospective adopters, adoptive parents and foster carers.

Catholic Child Welfare Council
www.vois.org.uk/cathchild
Catholic Child Welfare Council provides services for adopted people and others formerly in their care, including child migrants.

ACKNOWLEDGEMENTS

The publisher is grateful for permission to reproduce the following material.

While every care has been taken to trace and acknowledge copyright, the publisher tenders its apology for any accidental infringement or where copyright has proved untraceable. The publisher would be pleased to come to a suitable arrangement in any such case with the rightful owner.

Chapter One: An Overview

Adoption – some questions answered, © British Agencies for Adoption & Fostering (BAAF), *Adoptions*, © Office for National Statistics (ONS), *Age groups*, © Office for National Statistics (ONS), *Adoption, fostering and residential care*, © Catholic Child Welfare Council, *Thinking about adoption*, © Adoption UK, *Access to birth records*, © 1998-99 Crown Copyright, *The Adoption Contact Register*, © 1998-99 Crown Copyright, *Number of adoptions*, © Office for National Statistics (ONS), *What is the Adoption Information Line?*, © Adoption & Fostering Information Line? (AFIL), *Disabled people adopting children*, © Adoption & Fostering Information Line (AFIL), *Adopting a disabled child*, © Adoption & Fostering Information Line (AFIL), *Action taken to achieve right balance for adoption*, © 1998-99 Crown Copyright, *Adopting from overseas*, © 1998-99 Crown Copyright, *Role of the Department of Health Adoption Unit*, © 1998-99 Crown Copyright, *Overseas Adoption Helpline*, © Overseas Adoption Helpline.

Chapter Two: The Adoption Debate

Take adoption away from local authorities says report, © The Institute of Economic Affairs (IEA), *Adoption procedure 'is failing children'*, © Telegraph Group Limited, London 1998, *'Anti-adoption culture' to be investigated*, © The Independent, March 1999, *Councils named in adoption crisis*, © The Independent, April 1999, *The worst authorities*, © House of Commons, *This adoption scandal*, © The Daily Mail, April 1999, *Adoption row over teenage mothers*, © Vikram Dodd, January 1999, *Adoption*, © Melanie Phillips/Angela Neustatter, January 1999, *Couples barred from adopting children of a single mother*, © The Daily Mail, March 1999, *Adoption by single people*, © British Agencies for Adoption & Fostering (BAAF), *One parent is enough*, © The Daily Mail, February 1999, *Secrets, lies and the burning need to discuss adoption*, © The Independent, January 1999, *I hope Sally doesn't hate me*, © Telegraph Group Limited, London 1998, *TALKadoption*, © TALKadoption, *The mother of all meetings*, © Telegraph Group Limited, London 1998, *Babies' four-year wait for adoption*, © The Independent, October 1998, *A case of mixed blessings*, © Sarah Wellard, April 1999, *A question of trust*, © Henrietta Bond, April 1998.

Photographs and illustrations:

Pages 1, 5, 14, 15, 21, 22, 24, 33, 36: Pumpkin House, pages 7, 12, 19, 20, 29, 39: Simon Kneebone.

Craig Donnellan
Cambridge
September, 1999